re:FOCUS

Patrick A. Hegarty

SPIRITANDTRUTH.NET.AU

AUSTRALIA

Copyright © 2018 Patrick A. Hegarty.

1st Edition
ISBN: 978-0-6483391-3-7

All rights reserved. No part of this publication may be reproduced, distributed or transmitted in any form or by any means, including photocopying, recording, or other electronic or mechanical methods, without the prior written permission of Patrick Hegarty, except in the case of brief quotations embodied in critical reviews and certain other non-commercial uses permitted by copyright law. For permission requests, email the author, with subject line "Attention: Permissions Enquiry" at the email address below.

admin@spiritandtruth.net.au
www.spiritandtruth.net.au

Scriptures quoted from: New International Version of the Bible. Scripture taken from the Holy Bible, NEW INTERNATIONAL VERSION®. Copyright ©1973, 1978, 1984 International Bible Society. All rights reserved throughout the world. Used by permission of International Bible Society.

Scripture quotations identified MSG are from The Message. Copyright © 1993, 1994, 1995 by Eugene Peterson. Used by permission of NavPress Publishing Group.

Any internet addresses (websites, blogs, etc.) in this book are offered as resources. They are not intended in any way to be or imply an endorsement by Patrick Hegarty, nor does Patrick Hegarty vouch for the content of these sites for the life of this book.

Acknowledgements

HAVING WRITTEN TWO OTHER books on this subject of God's calling, and having facilitated many retreats with the readers, I want to thank the many hundreds who have shared their stories and experiences of living it out.

By listening to and watching the organic and sometimes chaotic journeys of God's people, I have learned that you can't come close to constraining the ways of God to a book. We authors love clear principles and axioms, and they have their place. But these people have taught me that undefinable faith and mystery play a huge part in God working His way through the mess of our life.

Thanks and acknowledgment also go to author and friend Malcolm Webber. His writings on the simplicity of Jesus' method for growing people provide a great model for understanding how God takes us on a journey of calling. His simple "5C" structure for development goals provided inspiration for the framework used in this book. Find his material at *www.leadersource.org*.

Contents

Introduction vii

Group Session 1   1

WEEK 1 – DEPTH OF CALLING

Depth of calling 11
A need to re:FOCUS 19
Impressive or impacting 27
Life in God's garden 35
Walking and working in the garden 43
The relational rhythm 51

Group Session 2   59

WEEK 2 – RE:FOCUS ON CHRIST

First 65
Getting derailed 73
Abiding 81
Changing lenses 89
re:FOCUS on Christ 97
Living from Christ 105

Group Session 3   113

WEEK 3 – RE:FOCUS ON CHARACTER

I have made you 119
Stuck in a moment 127
Growing character 135
The fruit of perseverance 143
The wilderness effect 151
re:FOCUS on character 159

Group Session 4   167

WEEK 4 – RE:FOCUS ON PEOPLE

People are your purpose 173
Your area of influence 181
You and the church 189
Oikos 197
Your tribe 205
re:FOCUS on people 213

Group Session 5   **221**

WEEK 5 – RE:FOCUS ON TALENT

re:FOCUS on talent 227
Put your soul into it 235
The heart speaks 243
The need at hand 251
Spiritual gifts 259
When doing it for God is not enough 267

Group Session 6   **275**

WEEK 6 – RE:FOCUS ON CALLING

re:FOCUS on calling 281
What is the purpose of all this? 289
Whose I am 297
Who am I becoming? 303
Who are mine? 309
What have I got? 313

Group Session 7   **319**

A PLAN TO RE:FOCUS

re:FOCUS on God: *Knowing Whose I am* 327
re:FOCUS on Character: *Cultivating who I am becoming* 331
re:FOCUS on People: *Influencing those around me* 335
re:FOCUS on Talent: *Giving it everything I have got* 339
Other important areas in which to re:FOCUS 343

Introduction

ONE OF THE QUESTIONS most frequently asked by a Christian is, "What are you calling me to do, God?"

We long for our life to count for something. We want to be doing what our Lord wants us to do. We do not want to make a mistake or wrong turn and possibly lose years.

We want clear direction, and yet most of our stories seem incredibly messy, even confused. For some, this most frequent prayer seems to be the least frequently answered!

Often that is because we are asking God the wrong question. He wants to talk at least as much about who He calls you to *be* as what He calls you to *do*.

You might want Him to give you a map. He intends to give you a compass.

The modern 21st-century world conspires to blur the vision of sincere believers. By focusing our eyes on fulfilling an impressive destiny or observable success, we can lose sight of the greater prize—the extension of God's kingdom, one person at a time.

We need a reminder of what it is we are here for. We need to find a way to keep our eyes fixed on what matters, both now and in eternity. We need to clear our vision of materialism and individualism.

We need to refocus.

This book is a change from emphasising the conventional checklist of personality type, spiritual gift inventory and skill set to define your calling. Instead, you will discover who you are called to be within the changing seasons and even occasional chaos of life.

Our situations are seldom clear cut or consistent. Circumstances change suddenly, job markets move around, relationships shift and priorities morph with age. It is impossible to determine in advance what your long-term life direction is when so many variables come at you. You are not some set-and-forget toy robot that God winds up and releases in the right direction.

God's purposes for you are so much deeper than that. He calls you first to Himself, then to the world. He calls you to be like Him and then to live from Him. He has wired you to have faith that will lead to unique deeds.

This book will take you on a journey to discover and implement a new depth to your calling. Something deeper than knowing which job to take or what ministry to serve in.

You will look at God's eternal purpose and how your life fits in to that. You will discover how to first immerse yourself in God, and then the people around you that He has called you to impact. With those profound dynamics in place, you will then consider the needs of the world around you and how you are uniquely equipped to make a difference.

By the end of the book you will have formed a working vision of a preferred future, a description of your calling to live out God's purpose in this season.

If, at the end of that, you are still asking "What's next, Lord?", then the answer will probably come much more quickly and clearly.

For more than a decade and half, I have had the privilege of pastoring God's people and authoring material that has equipped thousands for transformation and fruitfulness. The huge majority of those people have experienced significant breakthrough and increase in effective mission as they have applied the principles you find in this book.

Many have gone on to birth ministries, impact workplaces and create charities. Others have invested more fruitfully in their local church or sought out mission fields. Still more have simply increased in their ability to hear and respond to God's voice in their daily situation, praying for the sick and sharing the gospel.

Much of what you will read is an application of the principles and stories from scripture. You will look at many characters as they moved through life under the direction and formation of their God. You will recognise many of their dilemmas in your own life, and how God used these dilemmas to refine their calling.

You don't need a more detailed road map for life. You need a deeper relationship with the life-giver. It is from Him that guidance, priority and power come to fulfil His will.

God is calling you. Are you courageous enough to refocus on what He is saying?

Patrick Hegarty

Using this material

MEET TOGETHER WEEKLY

This material is designed to be done with others. There are six readings per week, followed by a group session. Group sessions are great settings to share and process your responses to daily content.

DIGEST THE CONTENT DAILY

Read a single chapter per day, and invest time thinking about your response. Read the scripture verses mentioned at the beginning of each chapter, before working through each day's content.

ATTEND A SPIRITUAL RETREAT

Completion of chapter 2.6 (ending week 2) is an effective moment to run a spiritual retreat. There participants can pause to receive ministry, and process deeply the concepts before contemplating change. Resources for hosting a spiritual retreat are available at *www.spiritandtruth.net.au*.

Group Session 1

INTRODUCTIONS

Spend some time going around the group, hearing the names, family details and life context of each participant.

Q. What would you like to get from this course?

_____

_____

ABOUT RE:FOCUS

Read together:

Welcome to re:FOCUS. This course is to equip you in taking up your calling in Christ.

Dwell on that statement for a moment. As a believer, your calling is only found in Christ. To be *in* Christ your calling must come *from* Him, be fueled *by* Him, and be fulfilled *for* Him. What that means is, your calling is not just about you!

For us to discover and walk in God's plan for us we must see beyond ourselves and refocus on the things that matter in

God's overall vision. It is when we choose to alter our focus in this way, that new possibilities open up.

Group agreement

For your group to be safe and effective, you will need to agree on how you will interact and honour each other. Talk through together which boundaries you may want to have in place for the duration of the course. Below are some suggestions and you can add your own.

Group attendance

We will honour each other by being on time and regularly attending meetings.

Safe environment

We will create a place where each person is protected and loved, free to share without judgment or unsolicited advice.

Respect differences

We will be gentle and gracious to those with different spiritual maturity, opinions and temperaments.

Confidentiality

What is said in the group stays in the group.

Faithfulness

We will diligently engage with the material, processing our responses honestly.

OTHER POINTS OF IMPORTANCE

Are you ready to fly?

Read together the *Parable of the Butterfly* (pg. 7).

Q. Do you see any parallels between the butterfly's shift in vision, and that of believers who determine to look past their own needs and capacities to that of God's grander design?

_____

_____

_____

Q. What do you hope to gain from engaging in this course? What are you looking for regarding the discovery of your calling?

_____

_____

_____

Read together:

You might have thought that the caterpillar represents the unredeemed version of a person, and that the butterfly is the new believer. Not so!

1 Corinthians 2:14 – 3:1 defines three states of spiritual maturity that we must traverse:

- **Natural person** (Gk: *Psuchikos*) – a person who is without the Spirit. An unredeemed person.
- **Carnal person** (Gk: *Sarkikos*) – a person who is redeemed, yet immature. Led by the old-nature.
- **Spiritual person** (Gk: *Pneumatikos*) – a person who is predominantly led by the Spirit. A mature believer.

The caterpillar represents the carnal believer. One who has their sights set on their own desires. A true morphing takes place when a believer matures to become led by the Spirit. It is a common next step for them to consider how they can best steward their life to fulfill God's plan. The butterfly represents a spiritual person such as this.

Q. Before you begin reading the course material, try to articulate to the group how you see your calling in Christ. How would you define it? What do you know, and what is missing about what He wants you to be and do?

_____

_____

_____

_____

_____

_____

Pray for each other

Take some time discussing the prayer needs of each person in the group and how best you will support them through this course.

_____

_____

_____

_____

_____

_____

_____

_____

_____

Finish the meeting by having the group all stand in a circle. Then take turns having the others lay hands on them, praying that God would answer their prayers and hopes.

The Parable of the Butterfly

For the brand-new butterfly, it was like there were two realities in her mind that had no connection to each other.

One was past, a shadow. She remembered days crawling on a single small branch simply eating. There was nothing to do except satisfy the desire to consume. Neither her view or interest went beyond that branch, or even the next leaf. But, why would she want to see further than that anyway?

But now she was altogether new. She had these brand-new wings – and she was so uplifted physically and spiritually that she didn't dwell on why it came so naturally to fly as she could. Life now looked completely different, even though her old branch remained below.

Now she could see life beyond the branch to the broad and unconstrained expanse of the garden. This was her new reality and there were no limits here. The garden had always existed of course, she just couldn't see it. Her vision had been constrained and blurred, and her desires focused on that insatiable desire for more.

But now she had to refocus.

A change of perspective had been thrust upon her and life would never look the way it did before. It would be unthinkable to have the gift of flight and yet choose to crawl. She needed to learn how to be compelled by a higher calling now, instead of carnal desire.

Soon she would learn what that calling was.

She was destined to find joy in the garden and be the source of joy for others. She was to know freedom and enjoy fruitfulness. Her story was to be part of something larger than her. She would learn to enhance the garden and enjoy knowing the Gardener.

It was time for her to answer the call to fulfill her design.

Week 1

Depth of Calling

There is more to this life than you may think.
God calls you deeper and sends you wider
as you discover a new rhythm of grace.

1.1

Depth of calling

> Calling is primarily about living *from* God, not living *for* God in your own strength. You are called to something deeper than merely doing.

READ FIRST: GENESIS 2

Human beings have always been attracted like moths to the flame of purpose.

Life is valuable and short and we want to make it count. We long for that sense of meaning and occasional elation that comes from reaching a significant milestone or doing something that matters to humanity. We don't want our life to be wasted or worthless.

For those who follow Christ, we long to fulfil His design for our life, without missing a single waypoint on our journey.

But what are those waypoints?

How will I know them when I see them? Do I stop at every crossroad until a light goes green, or are those lights already green, leaving me the freedom to choose which way to go?

Christian people often struggle with these issues, even more than unbelievers. Ours is not an individualistic worldview. We are not alone and without accountability. We are not simply making choices without consequences or a moral grid.

We have God to consider and to partner with!

We want to live for Him and with His guidance. We want Him to be involved in what we do and why. We want Him to show us which way to go, leading us in paths that hopefully avoid trouble and meaninglessness.

And yet that guidance can seem troublingly inconsistent. At times He is clear, opening a door we never could and shining a light on our next steps. But just as often He is quiet, seeming to force us into figuring things out in other ways. He may choose for us to hear Him through the wisdom of another person's advice. At other times we sense a deafening silence that compels us to choose a path for ourselves based on our morality and wisdom.

God is consistent, but His dealings with us are not. They adjust for every situation, season of life and stage of our maturity. His role is not to make our decisions for us but to grow us in maturity, faithfulness and, ultimately, fruitfulness. Rather than carry us as infants, there is a time when He must train us to crawl, walk and eventually to run.

This type of spiritual growth is seldom a comfortable experience. Every new level is brand new to us, with unchartered experiences and emotions.

Early on in our walk, God's open doors might have seemed easily identified by the way things fell in to place and blessing followed. But later, things aren't so clear. Many disciples make a sacrificial call to follow a path God has called them on, only to find incredible hardship and little confirmation by way of results or encouragement.

It is tempting to respond with, "Lord, did I miss it? Did I turn right when you turned left?"

How do you know when you are living within God's call for your life? Are circumstances the indicator, or is there something else?

What is God's call anyway? Is it a set of specific tasks to accomplish? Is it a matter of doing an inventory of your spiritual gifts and personality and plugging them into a church ministry? Or could it be something deeper—something beyond simply doing things?

Yes. God's call on your life is much more profound than a string of things you should do. And whilst being functional in life is not wrong, it is just not the whole story. Our function is to be derived from a sense of fullness: we give from what we receive; we do because of who we are.

Being is the source of doing.

God's calling on your life starts with who you are and whose you are, not what you do. He designed you with a certain architecture—you are spirit, soul and body. Ultimately, God also wove into you a unique set of characteristics, and a place in time and space to invest them. But to ignore our architecture, and instead focus on using personal characteristics like some personal toolbox, will rob your heart of its significance and lead to a shallow and functional life.

When you thrive at being, your doing will naturally bear great fruit. When you know who you are, you enquire less about what to do. You do what is consistent with your identity and purpose.

The model given in the Garden of Eden shows both the fullness and root of our calling. In that original setting, we can see how *being* produced *doing*, and how the doing was able to change the world for the better.

It all begins with God. His nature determined ours, since humanity was crafted in His image. There is a uniqueness about us—we have a heart that yearns for eternity and meaning. We are creative, having an eye for beauty. We are inventive, harbouring a yearning for progress and challenge.

We alone had the breath of God infused into our lungs—a lifelong reminder that He fuels our existence from His proximity and power. This facet alone—the breath of God within us—differentiates us most clearly from any other creature. We are designed to literally live from God.

But can you see how different living *from* God is to living *for* God?

When we ask, "What is my calling?" we are usually trying to define what we can do for God. There is nothing wrong with that; it is what we call faithfulness. But faithfulness without faith is hollow and often powerless. Faith relies on God. It requires Him to be engaged, giving us what we cannot give ourselves.

To live from God means that his grace, love and power so permeate my being that they overflow into what I do. Like a mountain lake being constantly filled by melting snow, a stream of living water inevitably breaks out to bring life wherever it goes.

God's grace, though, is not some impersonal force. It is His empowering presence, the reality of God Himself being with us as close as the air we breathe. He is always there, dwelling within. But just as we can choose to be emotionally close or distant from family and friends who share our physical space, so we can disconnect from this God who is with us.

Communion with God is the primary element to our calling. Everything else that we are and do hinges on this one dynamic.

Eden shows us where this design began. Dust and breath combined to define human life, and that is how it is meant to continue. Our calling is deeper than doing something *for*

God—it is becoming someone *through* God and, ultimately, living *from* God.

This principle is incredibly simple and yet remains one of the most elusive dynamics of the Christian life. We are accustomed to autonomy and independence. We want to be faithful, and yet do it alone. We don't know instinctively how to engage with God in a way that produces the fruit Jesus talked about in John 15.

Look how it played out in the life of Simon Peter. Between his initial call from Christ to follow and the three-fold denial of their relationship after the last supper, Simon had tried and failed at almost everything his bravado attempted. His strength counted for nothing.

After Jesus rose and eventually gathered the disciples around a breakfast of fish, the anticipated moment of reckoning came for Simon in John 21. But instead of rebuke, it was a beautiful illustration of the how and what of his future leadership.

"Do you love me Simon?"

"Yes, Lord."

"Then feed my sheep."

It was to be the love Simon had for Christ that made feeding the sheep possible. Simon (a name meaning *wispy reed*) would grow to become Peter (the *rock*) through the power of his relationship with Christ. Calling is not about what we do, but who we are and whose we are.

In the pages to follow you will discover the depth and ultimate purpose of your calling. If you are prepared to step out of the mindset of independence and into the world of partnership with God, you will, as Paul encouraged, "Live a life worthy of the calling you have received" (Ephesians 4:1).

PRAY:

Lord, take me from function to fullness!

Take me from a desire for direction, to a hunger for connection.

Show me your ways, so I can find myself in you. Amen.

YOUR RESPONSE:

How have you defined what God's calling would look like for you? Does this chapter change that? How?

_____

_____

_____

_____

_____

1.2

A need to re:FOCUS

We need God's help and His perspective
to see our calling as we should.

READ FIRST: 2 KINGS 6:8–18

The kingdom of God never advances in the same way that the empires of this world do.

The king of Aram, we observe in 2 Kings 6, was doing what men like him do; they take ground from their neighbours by force and then enslave or destroy the population. It was all part of a king's employment contract in those days. But Israel had a man of God in their corner, warning his own leader of the enemy's movements. In response, the king of Aram sent an overwhelming force to shut Elisha down.

When Elisha's servant saw the force surrounding them, he lost focus.

Up until that point, the servant probably had faith that God was smart enough to give prophetic words to Elisha, and would even be willing to save Israel. It hadn't occurred to him that God was concerned enough to save him personally.

This mindset is also common among God's people today. We have heard stories of miraculous intervention, and perhaps even prayed for people, believing that God can do anything. But we are not so sure He would do it for us.

Our focus is too easily drawn to our own problem, not the power of God and His grace to save.

Elisha prayed that his servant's eyes would be opened—that he might focus on the greater reality, not an inferior one.

Paul once prayed a similar thing for us:

> *"That the eyes of your heart may be enlightened in order that you may know the hope to which he has called you, the riches of his glorious inheritance in his holy people, and his incomparably great power for us who believe"* (Ephesians 1:18–19).

God's plan often remains invisible to us without the help of His Spirit to reveal it. And so, in penning scripture, Paul provides a theologically legal blueprint for us to adopt—ask God to open our eyes!

And what God reveals to us are two things, which become the basis of our hope-filled calling: our inheritance as believers, and the power available to us to fulfil His plan.

Normally, when we ask God the question, "What are you calling me to do?" we are looking for specific direction. We want a door to open or close, or a signal to be given to turn right or left. But since we are sons, not slaves, God speaks to us in the language of powerful inheritance, not binary directions.

However, if the only language we understand is that of a slave, we will simply not discern His guidance. In fact, we will probably hear nothing at all!

Slaves only do what they are told. They are not allowed to think for themselves, or invest as partners in the household. Sons, in a spiritual and non-gender based sense, are also heirs—they steward the family inheritance. Look at how Paul describes it:

> *The Spirit you received does not make you slaves, so that you live in fear again; rather, the Spirit you received brought about your adoption to sonship. And by him we cry, 'Abba, Father'.*
>
> *The Spirit himself testifies with our spirit that we are God's children. Now if we are children, then we are heirs—heirs of God and co-heirs with Christ…* (Romans 8:15–17).

In the setting in which Paul was writing, an heir was a child, usually a son, who had proven themselves able to handle the responsibilities of the family business. It was not an issue of the parents dying and leaving the inheritance, as it is in our culture. Usually the parents were still alive and they would hand over the family business so the heir could grow it to the benefit of all. Often the parents would still provide guidance and resource, but their assistance was to be invited by the functioning heir.

As a believer, the presence of God's Spirit within us qualifies us as heirs of God's kingdom. We get to grow the family business!

That is your calling in its simplest terms—to live in and advance the kingdom of God. And this is completely reliant on the presence and ongoing empowerment of God's Spirit. We need the Spirit to enlighten us (Ephesians 1:18–19), and we need the Spirit to empower us (Romans 8:15–17).

The ramifications of this are immense for the way we view and live out our days.

It stands to reason that whatever we do that does not require the Spirit's help is probably of no use in God's kingdom. Jesus could not have been clearer in this regard when He said, "... apart from me you can do nothing" (John 15:5).

And yet, you and I know that there are lots of things we can do without tapping in to God's power. We can sin, we can overwork and we can be slothful, to name a few. It is just that none of these things will be fruitful or advance God's work because they are outside of His plan and power.

If we want to do something that matters forever, then we will need God's input. If He is calling us to do or to be anything, the prerequisite will be the element of impossibility. His call is a partnership and, as such, will require the input of both partners.

When we pray with the posture and language of a spiritual slave, we will only perceive answers of precise direction, or rebuke. In reality, God sees us as children and heirs, with the freedom to choose. He then empowers those godly and wise choices that honour His kingdom. As a loving Father helping His children grow, He encourages us to practise the power and authority He has already given, rather than plead as if it is absent.

To walk in that calling, we need to refocus.

Rather than paying primary attention to the forces arrayed against us and to our apparent helplessness, we should focus on what God has provided and how to steward that.

When we lose that focus, everything quickly gets blurry. Time and again through the gospels we see Jesus teaching the disciples to refocus beyond what they see, to what was theirs by inheritance.

In Mark 8:17, the twelve had just witnessed the feeding of the four thousand and, not long previously, the five thousand. But as they got in the boat to leave, they realised there was only one loaf for their own lunch and began to focus on that. Jesus said, "Why are you talking about having no bread, do you still not understand?" Their logic was centred on the blurred vision of one loaf and not on what Jesus had just demonstrated was possible: feeding thousands.

Blurred vision does this to us. All we can see is what we do not have, rather than what is available to us. We pray desperately for more of God, and yet He is already fully with us. We plead with Him to change our circumstance, when He has already promised to overcome any circumstance from within.

Blurred vision no longer sees potential, it only recognises problems. So we begin reminding God of our apparent hopelessness and desperation, detailing a long list of problems we need Him to solve. Like Simon Peter, we tell Jesus to get rid of the hungry crowds. But, speaking from the logic of inheritance, Jesus says, "You feed them" (Matthew 14:16).

If we have blurred vision during the storms of our life, we wake up God with our prayers saying, "Can't you see I am about to drown?" But He questions us in return with, "Where is your faith?" expecting us to use our authority to bring peace (Matthew 8:26).

Jesus rightly expects the impossible of us, assuming we are learning to partner with His "incomparably great power" (Ephesians 1:19). He even taught us how to pray from that inheritance: "Your kingdom come, your will be done, as it is in heaven" (Matthew 6:10).

This is a prayer of kingdom focus. Instead of seeing things from the earth's point of view, reminding God of all the problems He already knows exist down here, we are to look from heaven's standpoint at what could and should be. Our calling is to make earth look more like heaven, in partnership with the Spirit who makes God's will possible.

God has given you a very different set of lenses to wear. Most of the people you interact with day to day will not have them, but you do. Will you choose to see things as God does, and how He invites you to see them?

Pray:

Lord, open my eyes to see the way you do!

Help me see beyond problems, to see what is possible.

Show me the inheritance you have for me to steward.

Release in me the power of your Spirit to fulfil your calling on my life.

Amen.

Your response:

What problem in your life might be better seen as an opportunity or possibility for God to do a work for the kingdom?

_____

_____

_____

_____

_____

1.3

Impressive or impacting

Solomon looked back at life from a palace, Paul from a prison. Which life and legacy would you choose?

READ FIRST: ECCLESIASTES 1:1–18

Solomon had been groomed to experience and extend the limits of humanity.

Raised in a house of privilege and power, called by God, imbued with incredible insight and entering his prime just as his nation was at its all-time zenith, his was always going to be a story to be remembered.

But what would that story be?

More to the point, would Solomon's story be one of impact?

His life and persona were incredibly impressive. All the elements were in place to give the opportunity for this one man's life to change the world. He had long held a top-5 spot on the world's most rich and famous list. His armed forces intimidated nations. He was wise and had political connections throughout the known world.

However, being impressive did not equate to having impact.

Most of us equate significance with being impressive to those around us. In this age of selfies and celebrity, perception and self-promotion are king.

We are led to think we must raise ourselves higher, do better, think smarter, look younger, go faster and be noticed more often.

Solomon did all that, but in the end he could not reconcile this experience of life's outer limits with his feelings of futility and deep depression.

That is because the human spirit does not thrive on success, but on significance. The momentum of Solomon's pursuits had led him beyond the fence of godly morality and humility. And the wider his boundary of experience went, the shallower he found its meaning.

In his folly, he would finally conclude that "It is all meaningless, a chasing after the wind".

It might be hard for you to imagine what was going on in Solomon's mind as he wrote that. How could he possibly have achieved and possessed so much and yet summarise life's pursuits so negatively?

He was articulating the emptiness of self-gratification.

Like an addiction to junk food, it's possible to consume vast amounts from life yet demand ever more. Solomon said that "The eye never has enough seeing, nor the ear its fill of hearing". We see it in our day as well. A person with no significant problems can still become depressed and suicidal. A "high-achiever" still becomes envious of those who have gone further, and frustrated at those who cannot keep up.

Solomon was right, at least in part. So much of our life's pursuits are meaningless. Even if you win the rat race, you are still a rat.

Woven into us by God is a longing for something else. Something eternal—something holy.

A life of impact.

But look closely at that word *impact*. To impact people means you have engaged with them and affected their lives. You have left a mark and it will stay with them. Your presence has changed the life of someone, and your existence continues to ripple out, possibly to generations.

However, for them to change does not always require you to be noticed. You can be impacting without being impressive.

Success, in a worldly sense, usually comes with a degree of visibility and recognition. We impress, and with that might come a degree of useful credibility, providing a platform for impact if we use it well.

However, the humblest and least impressive person can still have impact. Indeed, we can change the world without anyone knowing who we are. We can be secure enough in our identity to not be noticed, but focused enough to do what really matters. This is a life of significance.

You may have heard of the term *butterfly effect*.

The idea is that a major weather event such as a hurricane can be affected in location or strength by the cumulative consequences of many other minute events. Weeks earlier a butterfly beyond the horizon flapped its wings and a breath of turbulence moved a leaf. An insect on that leaf jumped off, catching the attention of a bird who leaped forward for an easy meal. That in turn startled a flock of birds who took flight, setting off an even greater movement of air, which joined with a thousand other such random occurrences. The cascading effect of the butterfly's presence eventually changed the course of the hurricane, and the world looked very different.

The butterfly had impact, and yet no one noticed. Not even the butterfly! It was simply doing what it knew to do, in the way it was designed to do it.

And yet this was not always the case for the butterfly. As a caterpillar, it had no ambition to fly even though the ability was woven deep within it, yet to be unleashed. It was self-consumed and short-sighted.

The spiritual parallel for this can be seen in our own journey with Christ. As we mature, we inevitably become aware of our responsibility to make a difference to the world. And yet, until we deal with the more carnal and "caterpillar-like" parts of our nature, our drive for meaning can lead us down destructive and self-gratifying paths.

As Paul explains thoroughly in Romans 8, we must live as mature, spirit-empowered people, not those controlled by our old nature. The dilemma we face, however, is that we can choose from moment to moment to be either a caterpillar or a butterfly! We can act maturely with self-control and spiritual fruit at church, but in the car on the way home we can lose our head at the slightest frustration.

This book is written for those who long to fly rather than crawl.

The offer to live from the Spirit to impact the world is ever-present, but many are unsure how to use their wings. Our only model has been to impress or to seek out success. We are encouraged if we get lots of likes on our latest social media post, but we secretly wonder what would get God's thumbs up.

Paul urges us in Ephesians 4:1 to "live a life worthy of the calling you have received".

He wrote that from a windowless prison cell, chained to a cold wall. And yet he still felt the thrill of fulfilling his calling. He could sing in the dark and pray for the saints with fervour and effect.

His sense of having God's thumbs up may have given some extra warmth to his soul. And yet Paul would have been happy enough without it. He didn't strive for repeated encouragement—he had long grown past that sort of need for affirmation. His joy and strength was found in God Himself—the relationship fueled his soul. In that sense, then, circumstances and opportunity were irrelevant for Paul.

Like the butterfly, Paul did what He was made to do, content to walk and work with God. The ramifications of his actions may have been big or small, but that was God's concern, not his. He knew that by partnering with His God he could affect more people with a single word or touch than a thousand men who worked in their own strength. Yet Paul was satisfied to impact one.

Consider the difference between the life and legacy of Paul and that of Solomon.

The world was impressed by Solomon for a moment. But the world is still being impacted by Paul two millennia later. At the end of their lives, one reflected back from a palace, the other from a prison. And yet it was the prisoner who was free and the king who had become a slave.

Solomon had lost focus; Paul saw more clearly with every year.

This book will help you refocus. It invites you to look at life differently—to get a clearer view of why you exist, and how to fulfil your calling in the way God designed you.

Whether you find yourself in a palace, a prison or anywhere in between, it is time for you to spread your wings.

Pray:

Lord, I thank you that I have been made to fly!

As I begin this journey of discovering my calling, show me your ways.

Take me to a place of impact, for the glory of your name alone.

Amen.

Your response:

Where has your focus been lately? Has it been on your own success, or that of others? Is there a focus of your time, energy and passion that needs to be redirected to a more fruitful and eternal cause?

_____

_____

_____

_____

_____

_____

_____

1.4

Life in God's garden

> Worldly goals don't correlate to a kingdom
> calling. To understand God's plan for you,
> we must go back to the beginning.

READ FIRST: GENESIS 1

How does a newly hatched butterfly know what to do with its new wings? She has never flown before. Neither has she had lessons or an example to follow.

Instinct. She just knows what to do.

Flight is written so deeply into her DNA that it comes completely naturally. Even while she crawled and ate in her previous life as a caterpillar, that code was already hard-wired in.

Most elements of your calling, too, have been written into you since conception. And yet, unlike a butterfly, you have a mind that thinks for itself. Instinct must compete with intellect, and much of our mind has been taught to think in an ungodly way. And this must be continually untaught, even though you are a new creation.

Since the moment of your salvation, permission and power was granted to walk and work fully in your identity as God's child. Paul made clear in both Romans 8:15 and Galatians 4:6–7 that the presence of God's Spirit within you is the indicator of your identity as God's heir.

Over the long term, however, it isn't the lack of God's power that is the problem, it is the lack of clear vision that holds us back. We are too often focused on the world's idea of a life worth living, and struggle to find an alternative that is motivating enough for us to exchange our years on earth to pursue.

The biggest challenge to engaging in the life God calls us to is not our brokenness, it is our lack of clarity in how a preferred future should look. Christians generally just do not know what to aim for!

We have plans for our career, family, retirement and finances. But how many people do you know who have a plan for their spiritual life? We do not have any idea how far we should reach in seeing God's kingdom come as it is in heaven.

There seems to be so few examples before us of people living from a heavenly perspective compared to those who are dedicated to worldly living, that we find it difficult to even imagine what it might look like.

Now and again, however, some of us do give it a go anyway.

We set a plan for behaviour, or generosity, or ministry involvement. Ironically though, no sooner do we form an admirable long-term and definable goal than "life" seems to conspire to make it impossible! If we didn't know better, we might think that heaven is playing some sort of game with us.

Then we read in Ephesians 3:20 that God wants to do more than we can ask or imagine, so we might think, "Why would I bother asking or imagining for some great outcome if God is beyond all that?"

The problem lies in our logic and the type of result we are aiming at.

We naturally reason in terms of outcomes and goals. We think of so many people being saved or so many dollars raised for a missionary. We want an ethical bill passed by the government or a new church building in place.

But, did you notice that Jesus never thought that way?

All those outcomes are admirable and worthy. And yet Jesus didn't seem to be concerned with them. He wasn't interested in overthrowing the godless regime that ruled Israel. Nor did he show ambition for removing Herod, a ruler who mercilessly killed his own people. He didn't try to influence the religious elite or build a new synagogue for the glory of God.

He had two aims in mind—to die on the cross and to equip the disciples. And even with the greatest mentor of all time, one of those guys didn't turn out too well. In fact, the eleven that were left still seemed a little under-cooked for ministry when Jesus sent them out in Matthew 28.

Despite that, Jesus' life did give a model for us to follow.

Looking at His example, however, many of us get tripped up in the context of Jesus' life. His setting in 1st-century Palestine is obviously nothing like ours. He had no possessions, no spouse or children, and no need to consider life into retirement. Beyond that, His unique call to go the cross does not need to be replicated.

In that sense, we don't need to be like Jesus the Messiah. He did His job and we do not need to do it again. And yet, we have been predestined to be conformed to the image of Jesus (Romans 8:29). Not in role description, but in character and *modus operandi*.

His life is both perfect theology and a perfect example. He set aside glory to live as we do, giving an example of how it can look when a human being lives from the power and perspective of heaven.

The real question to consider then is, "What would Jesus be like if Jesus was you?"

If Jesus was in your shoes, with your context and calling, how would that look? His energy and priority would be directed to quite a different balance of things, I expect. He wouldn't have many of the same concerns or distractions. Ambition to succeed would not drive Him and it is doubtful that He would invest a lot of time on social media.

He would be all about intimacy with God and proximity to people. Just as He was in 1st-century Palestine.

Jesus was called the *second Adam* by Paul in 1 Corinthians 15:47. And like the first Adam found in Genesis, Jesus often met with God in the garden. It is in this original garden, Eden, that we can find the purest template for our life as God's child and heir.

Jesus, the person, lived out the model of character and calling birthed way back then in Genesis 1 and 2, before the fall. If we put aside His specific assignment as Messiah, we can see there the core elements that make up the design and commission of us all. Having been born again of God's Spirit and reconciled fully to God, Eden's promise and design is available again to you.

To see and embrace that design fully, we need to change the way we think.

As products of the industrial and information revolutions, we think in terms of function and knowledge. We use machines as an example of peak performance, running ourselves permanently at peak capacity, rather than embracing rest and relationship. We view personal growth in terms of gaining new information, rather than expanding our character or intimacy with God.

Your calling is way more profound than that. It is not about numbers and qualifications. Nor is it about performance or job titles.

Your calling is about life—abundant life. A full and connected life. A life that Jesus made possible for you.

> *"I have come that they may have life, and have it to the full."* (John 10:10)

The Garden of Eden shows us that life. It is a life of inheritance. Adam and Eve didn't create it, but they were given the honour of tending and growing it by their Father. God created for them a place to thrive and be fruitful. He even wove into them the desire to advance His kingdom of shalom into a world that was, as yet, uncultivated. They were to take Eden "out there".

The fundamental prerequisite that made it all possible was their deep communion with God. They were not just dust, formed from a physical substance to feed off that same substance. They were breathed into by God, His very presence as close as each subsequent breath.

To be fully human, we must be both dust and breath. Unlike the rest of creation, we bear God's image and have His Spirit as the Source of life. This reality has implications for almost every part of our life.

Our calling is completely reliant from moment to moment on our ability to live from the power and intimacy of our relationship with God. Anything done for God, without help from God, will be fruitless and exhausting. It is called religion! But this is the way most of us live, most of the time.

Your true purpose for life is found by embracing the inheritance of life in God's garden.

It is a life of relationship and resource, of power and of purpose. It is the life you are called to participate in for eternity, with God as your joy and reward.

Pray:

Lord, take me back to your garden!

I want to breathe in your presence and find peace in your purpose for me. Show me where I might have stepped out of that place, and how to leave behind the ways of the world that distract me from where you have designed me to be.

Amen.

Your response:

At this early stage of the book, how would describe the abundant life Jesus offered? Has any of it been a reality to you? Are there other facets you long for?

_____

_____

1.5

Walking and working in the garden

We are called to both faith and deeds, but both must be fueled by our relationship with Christ.

READ FIRST:

"Are you tired? Worn out? Burned out on religion? Come to me. Get away with me and you'll recover your life. I'll show you how to take a real rest. Walk with me and work with me—watch how I do it. Learn the unforced rhythms of grace. I won't lay anything heavy or ill-fitting on you. Keep company with me and you'll learn to live freely and lightly." (Matthew 11:28–30, MSG)

In the text above, Jesus was talking to God-fearing people who were suffering from performance fatigue. Nothing quite erodes the soul like the vortex of perpetual, religious self-assessment.

Against the standard of the Torah, the Jewish "people of the land" to whom Jesus was talking were always coming up short. And the Pharisees made a point of telling them so.

Things have changed in our era. Thanks to the Reformation, our bias now is towards justification by faith alone. And yet faith is never alone. It is quickly followed by its own ramifications—works.

> "For it is by grace you have been saved, **through faith**—and this is not from yourselves, it is the gift of God—not by works, so that no one can boast. For we are God's handiwork, created in Christ Jesus to **do good works**, which God prepared in advance for us to do." (Ephesians 2:8–10, my emphasis)

Did you see that? Just when we thought we were free, there it is again, a seeming obligation to perform—to do good works! The reality is that believers of our day remain as tired and worn out as they did when Jesus walked the streets.

Jesus' antidote, however, was not to stop working; it was to work with Him. He calls His people into relationship. And from the strength that union brings, the works become fruit rather than obligation.

There is a growing movement of people wanting to escape a life of unproductive religious busyness. They often respond in one of two ways. Option one is to over-retreat, claiming a seven-day Sabbath. Rejecting visionary challenge, they see their church life primarily as a place of rest and support—a hospital for the spiritually broken.

Option two often takes the form of a sort of zealous missional movement that can at times sound a little "anti-church". They push harder, go further, and give even more. One response seeks rest, the other seeks progress. Both resist busyness for busyness' sake.

Whilst both responses can look and be valid, they can also mask the real problem and, ultimately, fall victim to it. The issue here isn't whether we stop or whether we go; it is whether we are with Jesus in both modes. Both options have their time and place, but they slip into error when they are experienced without Jesus.

Jesus called us to both walk and work, but the important sub-clause was to watch how He does it. He is the great teacher as well as the source of supply.

Two words matter most in how we are to live out our calling over the long term: *relationship* and *rhythm*.

Relationship is all about the way we personally abide in Christ, bearing fruit that lasts (John 15:5). But it is also about the very dynamics of that relationship and our identity in Him. God is both our loving Father and also Lord of the harvest. That means we are beloved children who live in rest, whilst also being responsible heirs who get to work.

Rhythm is all about living those two relational facets in a complementary and symbiotic way, rather than seeing them as polar opposites. And right here is the genius in Christ's call to both walk and work with Him.

When we rest in Him by faith, walking closely as beloved children, we can enjoy the relationship, grace and peace that come from that. We can take time to heal, re-charge, re-assess and reset our course.

When we get to work, serving God and the world to advance the kingdom, we experience the joy of expending His energy, and our own, on something that matters for eternity. We can join with Paul saying, "To this end I strenuously contend with all the energy Christ so powerfully works in me" (Colossians 1:29, NLT).

When we allow ourselves to embrace both modes—that of a child (walking, being) and that of an heir (working, doing), we can enjoy fully the benefits of both without the burden of guilt or obligation. Indeed, time spent in each mode will naturally fuel and motivate an activation of the other.

It is inconceivable that we could dwell intimately with God, hearing His heart and being empowered by His vision, but not wanting to respond with action. Being with God will always result in us doing something in His name.

It is also inconceivable that we could go in God's name, working in powerful ways that require His involvement, without allowing ourselves to rest, even as God did through the birth of creation.

And it is in that created order that we see relationship and rhythm—it was how we began and it remains God's Plan A for fulfilling your destiny.

This combination was woven into the very fabric of the created order. We see it most clearly in the Garden of Eden, where Adam would work purposefully through the day and would walk with God in the cool of the evening (Genesis 1:28; 3:8).

There was naming of the animals to be done, with Adam defining their nature and purpose with a descriptive word. The garden itself needed to be cultivated, with fruit and vegetables to be grown. And beyond that, the outside world was a blank canvas for humanity to develop and govern under God. They were free to invent, create and experiment with new ideas.

Can you imagine the communion Adam and Eve shared with God and each other in those early days? They would share stories about what had been accomplished and what might be possible in the future.

Incredibly, that is the kingdom calling you have access to now.

Jesus' death bought back access to God. Relationship and rhythm is back on the agenda for us. You are free to create and relate, to both extend the kingdom and retreat into His arms.

Now, in practice, each of us will lean more naturally to one of these dynamics than the other. We prefer to either "be" or "do", and to gather around us people of similar ilk.

Let's be clear, to grow in our calling is not a matter of focusing on skills and gifting alone. In many writings of our day we are encouraged to simply focus on our strengths and delegate tasks to others where we are weak. That is a valid approach in regard to what we do, but in regard to who we are we need to address our flaws. Ultimately, our calling and capacity will be totally constrained by the level of our character!

To grow, we need to engage intentionally with both the doing of an heir and the being of the child.

Whilst one of those relational modes might feel awkward, it is stretching that area that will ultimately unlock your capacity in the other! And both modes will, if experienced correctly, require you to push more deeply into union with Christ.

Never forget, it is the very presence of God in your heart that makes any of this possible. It is your relationship that gives power to the rhythm.

> "The Spirit himself testifies with our spirit that we are God's children. Now if **we are children, then we are heirs:** heirs of God and co-heirs with Christ…" (Romans 8:15–17, my emphasis)

Pray:

Lord, have I been living from my own strength, and not yours?

Show me if I have focused on my own preference without walking and working fully with you.

Lead me back into union with you as the Source of my life.

Amen.

Your response:

Has your life been both restful and productive? Describe where you are strong in both areas and if there is a correction that needs to be made.

I am strong in **walking** with God in these ways:

_____

_____

I am strong in **working** with God in these ways:

_____

_____

I need to correct that ratio by:

_____

_____

1.6

The relational rhythm

Without a close union with Christ, our personal strengths can leave us with less than half of our potential story.

READ FIRST: JAMES 2:14–26

"It's ok for you to be a person who likes to worship and pray ... but I like to get things done."

Have you ever heard a comment like that in the church world? Perhaps you have said it yourself.

We often put people into these types of boxes as they conveniently label our various biases. But polarised definitions can inadvertently turn into excuses for not adopting what should be common to all. It is one thing to be at either end of a spectrum, it is another to try to escape the foundational aspects of spirituality that we are all supposed to share.

James 2 is a clear call for the necessity of both faith and deeds in our life. Neither is optional and both are supposed to come quite naturally to a believer.

But both do not come naturally to us, do they?

The same issue that was present in the early church still exists today. Our bias to exercise either faith or deeds comes to the fore when we are not fueled by our relationship with God. Our old nature is happy enough to focus on one or the other.

Amazingly, you can worship and pray and still lack an empowered relationship with God. Or, you can work for Him and even operate in the power of His spirit and yet not be connected to Him personally.

This may seem nonsensical to you. It did to me.

But when I first saw a string of high-profile and obviously gifted leaders fall morally, I could see there was a disconnect somewhere. And when I watched the most overt and passionate worshipper in a church walk out on their spouse for no legitimate reason, I knew God was not fueling their inner world. You can have a form of either faith or deeds and still lack the true presence and power of God in your life.

I hope this is getting your attention. Gifting or personality does not equal character. It is character that determines spiritual maturity and also creates the eventual high-water mark for our true impact for God.

James clarifies the situation by inferring that a form of faith is not true faith. He says, "What good is it if a man claims to have faith, but has no deeds" (James 2:14). Claims aren't considered reality until they can be proven.

Claimed faith might be better termed an *understanding* of God, rather than an *active reliance* on God. It believes that God exists but does not rely on or access that relationship to sustain life. Hence James's reference to the demons believing—obviously they know God exists, but there won't be any demons in heaven!

True knowledge of God, the type that changes us, combines understanding with experience. It knows God personally rather than just knowing about Him theoretically.

Why is this point so vital in regard to your calling, you may ask.

Because you will never experience the fullness of your destiny unless your relationship with God remains the source of life. When your relationship is functioning as it should, those things that once stood as opposites somehow become symbiotic. Rather than faith and deeds being at opposing ends of a spectrum, they become mutually beneficial partners.

Faith and deeds should in practice form something of a two-step dance. The momentum of one step leads naturally to the next, and so on. The Greek word for this is *perichoresis*, used by many theologians to describe a sort of interlocking and closed dance of the trinity.

If faith and deeds fall out of their relational rhythm, they step on each other's toes and must separate. They can only exist together when the believer is in union with Christ.

Take faith for example—it is a reliance on God, based on His word and nature. But if that faith exists without a vital relationship and connection through the Spirit, then it reverts to being theoretical—potentially a belief system that we can be either talked in or out of. In reality, we aren't to merely know about God, we are to know Him by experience.

> *"And this is how we know that he lives in us: We know it by the Spirit he gave us."* (1 John 3:24)
>
> *"This is how we know that we live in him and he in us: He has given us of his Spirit."* (1 John 4:13)

Theoretical faith doesn't touch our hearts—it leaves us without passion and a desire to share God's love. We remain essentially deedless. Oh, we might still do some things, but we flame out too fast or act out of obligation. We are bereft of God's love, sounding more like a clanging cymbal than a long-playing instrument of God's melody (1 Corinthians 13:1).

True faith overflows with love from the God we are connected to—it can't help but produce deeds.

Our deeds cannot remain alone. They are not the final expression of our relationship with God, but provide a crucial pathway back to His heart.

Too often, it is the sacrificial life of service to God that results in burnout or compassion fatigue. We start out wanting to express our commitment to Him by volunteering for this or that, readily walking through the doors of opportunity that an enthusiastic believer is invited through. But soon, however, our growing list of commitments outstrips our ability to draw from God as the Source. Over time, many become jaded and cynical about church life, and perhaps even God Himself.

The very calling we receive from God can be our undoing if we try to do it without Him.

The failure begins when we start doing more than our relational connection with God can sustain. Ironically, our busyness might even take away from our times of prayer and worship, rather than driving us deeper into an exercise of faith. We enthusiastically do what is possible in our own strength and therefore lose the benefit of relying on God Himself to work through us.

Our deeds should require, and even drive us, to rely on Him even more, thus ensuring the relational rhythm continues. Like walking and working, this rhythm of grace is reliant on God's empowering presence to bear fruit that lasts.

Now, at this point, what we often do after gaining mental agreement with this principle is make a formula out of it. We form a checklist in our heads, trying to ensure all the vital elements are included in our lives. But soon enough, faith and deeds become merely commodities that we need to include in the recipe. We might factor in a time and space for each but miss the underlying reality that they are supposed to spring naturally from our walk with God.

But remember, even a clanging cymbal can have a rhythm. We call it religion—a set of beliefs and actions that are bereft of intimate and active relationship with God.

Our faith is to be relational faith—that of a child relying on their loving Father. We rest on Him, trusting Him for strength, comfort, identity and rest.

> *"And so we know and rely on the love God has for us. God is love. Whoever lives in love lives in God, and God in them."* (1 John 4:16)

Our deeds, too, are to be relational—doing what we see Him doing, saying what He is saying, just as Jesus Himself demonstrated. You can only live this way if you are connected with God Himself through a vibrant life in His Spirit.

They are the deeds of an heir, working closely with the Father to grow the family kingdom. We get involved, exerting our limited strength, and yet we know that nothing will come of it unless God's own power does the heavy lifting.

> *"To this end I strenuously contend with all the energy Christ so powerfully works in me."* (Colossians 1:29)

Ultimately, these two symbiotic and mutually feeding elements become so woven together that they cannot be separated. Faith is shown in deeds, and deeds require growing faith. Indeed, Jesus, when asked by the Pharisees to define the works that God expects of His people, replied:

> *"The work of God is this: to believe in the one he has sent."* (John 6:29)

Pray:

Lord, it's so easy to forget that it is all about you.

Help me to not replace our relationship with religion, or a life that has a form of godliness, but no real power. Teach me how to rest and believe in you more deeply. Teach me also how to work with you to do that which is impossible in my own strength.

Take me deeper into you.

Amen.

Your response:

Left to your own devices, are you more inclined to want to do things for God or enjoy time with God? Is there anything about your life that you would need to adjust in light of today's reading?

_____

_____

_____

_____

Group Session 2

Depth of calling

The first group of readings (1.1 through 1.6) sought to reset your perspective on what God has called you to do and be. Rather than self-fulfillment and self-reliance, we are called to pursue and rely on our union with Christ.

Q. What was your overall response to this week of readings?

_____

_____

Now, discuss together your responses from this week's teaching:

1.1 Depth of calling

Calling is primarily about living from God, not living for God in your own strength. You are called to something deeper than merely doing.

Q. How have you defined what God's calling would look like for you? Does this chapter change that? How?

1.2 A need to re:FOCUS

*We need God's help and His perspective
to see our calling as we should.*

Q. What problem in your life might be better seen as an opportunity or possibility for God to do a work for the kingdom?

1.3 Impressive or impacting

*Solomon looked back at life from a palace, Paul from a
prison. Which life and legacy would you choose?*

Q. Where has your focus been lately? Has it been on your own success, or that of others? Is there a focus of your time, energy and passion that needs to be redirected to a more fruitful and eternal cause?

1.4 Life in God's garden

*Worldly goals don't correlate to a kingdom calling. To understand
God's plan for you, we must go back to the beginning.*

Q. At this early stage of the book, how would describe the abundant life Jesus offered? Has any of it been a reality to you? Are there other facets you long for?

1.5 Walking and working in the garden

We are called to both faith and deeds, but both must be fueled by our relationship with Christ.

Q. Has your life been both restful and productive? Describe where you are strong in both areas and if there is a correction that needs to be made.

- I am strong in **walking** with God in these ways:
- I am strong in **working** with God in these ways:
- I need to correct that ratio by:

1.6 The relational rhythm

Without a close union with Christ, our personal strengths can leave us with less than half of our potential story.

Q. Left to your own devices, are you more inclined to want to do things for God or enjoy time with God? Is there anything about your life that you would need to adjust in light of today's reading?

Conclusion of the group meeting

In closing, pray for each other that Christ would give them clarity in their aspirations and motivations. Seek God for specific grace to guide and provide for where He wants to take each participant.

Week 2

re:FOCUS on Christ

When everything of purpose that you do comes from the union you have with God, you are living *from* Him not just *for* Him.

2.1

First

Our commitment to serve God should not outstrip our communion with God.

READ FIRST: REVELATION 2:1–7

Somehow the church at Ephesus had lost its way. Originally, they had been the shining example of how God's people can impact their city. But now that shine had been dulled.

In the 40 years between Paul's first conversions in Ephesus and the writing of Jesus' letter to the Ephesians in Revelation 2, they had lost love and replaced it with work. A third generation of believers was predominantly at the wheel now. The pioneers who had personally experienced miraculous revival and persecution had mostly died off. They had passed on their stories, beliefs and practices down the line, but inherited tradition and faith had proven inadequate.

It echoes so many other stories we might hear in, of all places, a relationship counsellor's office.

The typical couple had once yearned for each other, longing to simply be close. They would talk, dream and do anything that might bring the other joy. But over the years they inevitably busied themselves, assuming the communion they had found at first would never change. And rather than building new layers of depth and love, they built an increasingly demanding life, relying on the assumption of historical love to get them through.

Life can out-grow our love for people and God if love isn't intentionally grown with it.

We start to replace adoration with achievement. We may even point at our hectic schedule and say, "I am doing this for you!"

But our spouses, or our children or our God, for that matter, do not want our achievements if they rob us of connection.

Jesus said to the Ephesians, "I know your deeds, your hard work and perseverance". He could have added, "Good job! Thanks for that. But what I want is you".

He then goes on, saying, "You have forsaken the love you had at first. Consider how far you have fallen!"

Jesus is clearly saying that our works rate below our relationship—a long way below. It reminds us of Matthew 7:23 where He rebuked those who did things for God without having a relationship with Him, saying, "Depart from me, I never knew you".

Your relationship with God can withstand a lack of performance, but it cannot withstand a lack of personal communion. When considering your life and your calling to steward the identity God has given, you cannot simply check the box that says, "In right standing with God", and walk on.

Our developing calling is handcuffed to our growing relationship with Christ.

If the work of our apparent calling progresses but the depth of our walk with God does not, then we not only exhaust ourselves but we step out of His will. If we are out of God's will, then at that point we have missed His calling.

Like the Ephesians, we may still be on the path He called us to follow, but we have begun to go it alone. We are cut off from the Source that fuels genuine fruit. Plenty of people live this way. Doing the stuff, but without the supply.

I wonder if Paul saw this coming for the Ephesian church.

At the very peak of their fruitfulness, he wrote them an exhortation we know as the book of Ephesians. Seeing the growth in their maturity and impact, he felt the urgency to pray for them. He wanted their hearts to be full of God in a way that gave strength and continued to propel them forward.

In chapter 3:16–19, he prayed they would grasp the unbelievable capacity of God's love to empower their lives, hoping they would "know this love that surpasses knowledge— that you may be filled to the measure of all the fullness of God".

Did you get that? Living in the fullness of God is only found by knowing God's love fully.

The word Paul uses for "know" is *ginosko*, a term depicting knowledge gained by experience, not just theory. That is why it is a knowing that is beyond the capacity of human knowledge; it requires God to be involved!

By the time Jesus wrote to the new generation of leaders at Ephesus, the type of experience Paul described had become rare at Ephesus. Their Christian life was now more about hanging on, enduring hardship, doing good and getting theology right. Experience with God had been replaced by an experience of church.

Theoretically, the two cannot be separated. But, as you may have experienced, it is not unusual for believers to meet on Sunday, being immersed in church but without encountering Christ.

Jesus may well say to us all, "Consider how far you have fallen". In regard to our personal calling in Christ, it is our loving communion with Him that is to be pursued the most.

Calling is deeper and broader than what we do for God. There are other principles to consider, all of which rely on our relationship with Him to be active.

For example, God very seldom calls us to do something that we can accomplish without His help. That means our faith will be stretched and our own strength will be insufficient!

"Without me you can do nothing", Jesus said in John 15:5. "But, if we remain in Him, we will bear much fruit."

Disconnection from God, which is the opposite of remaining in Him, is our enemy's favourite strategy. And he uses Christian endeavour at least as much as worldly pleasure to draw us from our intimacy with God.

The process Satan uses is predictable and obvious when you have eyes for it.

The very passion for God that opened doors for us to serve in church or mission can be redirected down the path to disillusionment. We begin with a sincere love for God which inspires us to serve. We enjoy investing extra time leading a study or playing in the worship team. But over time, the scriptures, which were once the source of so much strength and joy, become a textbook we must draw knowledge from to feed others. Each verse becomes potential lesson fodder, rather than fuel for our soul.

We may even find that the Sunday church service that gave us joy and celebration becomes just another place of labour, where excellence becomes more of our focus than Christ does at that moment.

We believers just seem to naturally become ever busier. And so, the extra time and alternate spaces we need to rediscover God can be increasingly hard to source. Rather than facilitating growth, our commitment slowly starves us spiritually. In the end, so many of those who are key to the operation of our churches struggle against spiritual burnout, compassion fatigue and even loss of faith.

This need not be the case, however!

By ensuring that commitment does not outstrip communion, we can be sure our lives don't take extended steps that outpace our character. This may well slow the pace of advancement somewhat, but it makes the journey one of joy and longevity.

Jesus encouraged the Ephesian believers to return to the love they had at the beginning of their walk. We never outgrow love. It is not something to be assumed upon or neglected. He wants and requires us to continually fan the flame of desire for our Saviour.

Jesus is not our personal assistant who we call on for tasks that need doing. Nor is He a distant boss who leaves us alone to faithfully carry out our job description. The whole spiritual dynamic of the kingdom of God is built on the principles of proximity and passion.

He is always present, always awake, always ready to guide our next steps. But engaging with God requires us to pursue Him, and to want to do so. By seeking first the kingdom, we are seeking first the King.

The highest priority in discerning and carrying out your calling in Christ is to pursue a developing communion with Him. From that foundation, all else is possible and all priorities are aligned with His will.

Pray:

Lord, please show me how to grow in my relationship with you. May I not replace communion with activity, or worship with service. Return me to my first love.

Amen.

Your response:

What phrases would you use to describe your first love for Christ in terms of your relationship, worship and responses to Him when you first came to Christ?

_____

_____

_____

_____

_____

_____

_____

_____

2.2

Getting derailed

The two best questions to ask regarding our life's calling are: "Who am I?" and "Whose am I?"

READ FIRST: ACTS 9:1–18

Why might Christ have chosen to stop Saul of all people in his tracks, reveal Himself so powerfully and then use him for His purposes so profoundly?

Up until that moment, Saul was the single biggest threat to the cause of Christ. Why bless someone like him when so many more worthy candidates would have stepped up to the plate willingly? Saul was ungracious, violent, proud and apparently possessed by hatred. By any assessment or prediction, he was seemingly least likely of all people to advance the gospel.

So, why Saul? We find the answer in Acts 9:15: "This man is my chosen instrument to proclaim my name to the Gentiles and their kings and to the people of Israel".

Saul had been chosen since before time—he just didn't know it.

Oh, he had a sense of purpose alright. He was determined, ambitious and opportunistic. He seemed to know he was destined for something special and invested deeply into his passions. The trouble was that he had embarked on a set of rails that led him away from God's purpose for him.

It didn't feel like that to Saul, however. He was convinced that his cause was right and his methods were called for. He may even, at times, have looked to heaven and said, "I am doing this for you, are you proud?"

So, how could a man with a call to go one way be so determined to go another? Especially a man who, by all accounts, possessed a clear belief in God and a detailed understanding of scripture.

Disconnection from God, pure and simple.

Saul would have prayed religious prayers all his life, but it is doubtful that he was listening for a response. As a Pharisee, his spirituality and righteousness were measured completely by externals, not the heart. Their worldview was that if you looked good and did good, then you were good with God.

His life was certainly on a set of rails, the only set that mattered in his eyes. And he wanted to get as far along that track as he could. That was until God Himself threw a log across the track and derailed him.

It was the encounter with Christ, face to face as it were, that put Saul on a different path. He had known about God, but now he knew Him up close and personal. Christ was real, personal, powerful and concerned about a very different agenda than the one Saul was working on.

Our perspectives, priorities and plans all change when we are in close contact with God.

Without that connection, we drift. Like Saul, we might be about worthy-sounding ambitions, but they are usually focused on achieving something rather than saving someone. Our heart isn't connected to His, being continually softened to the needs of others, and being fuelled by love. Life becomes about doing great things in God's name, but having our back turned to Him as we do so.

Now and again, however, God will derail us.

It is not always as dramatic as Saul's experience. It doesn't have to be. For the majority us, we have merely drifted slightly off course. Not too far that a firm reminder, or probing scripture, won't get our hearts turning back on track.

They are moments of recalibrating the soul. By reconnecting with Christ, we also reconnect with meaning, value and rest. We realise that it is of far more worth to know who we are than to think we know what to do.

When coming to terms with our calling in life, we normally think in terms of function. We know that God is real and that

He has put us on earth for a reason. And so often, like Saul, we go to work at achieving the things that matter to us with all zeal.

It might be a career, raising a family, building a ministry or even a church. All things of immense value to the world. But these things can so easily take on a life of their own. That which is worth doing can take up the passion reserved for the One worth pursuing. And in doing so, we lose focus.

In the blur of life, we don't notice our slight turns towards excess. We become less likely to assess motives and more likely to overlook the needs of others. But when God shines the light on us, we, like Saul, stop in our tracks again.

We find ourselves asking, "What am I doing?"

It is a good question, and this is a pivotal moment to embrace. But rather than simply assessing our works, we should take that opportunity to go a little deeper. "What am I doing?" is a question of function. What I do is ultimately driven by who I am.

"Who am I?" is a question of form rather than function. It looks to my identity, purpose and unique design. Answering that question often propels people into a whole new level of focus and influence. They begin to know what they should do and what they should not do. It gives permission to say no to good opportunities and to confine their yes to the great ones.

However, this is a question an unbeliever can ask too. Anyone, evil or good, can look to their history, values and personality profile to determine their focus. Young Saul had, no doubt, answered his "Who am I?" question in a way that justified violence and unbridled ambition.

For the believer, there is a more central question, the answer to which becomes the root of all things—our reason why, and our motivation to fulfil our design.

That question is, "Whose am I?"

This is not only a question of Lordship; after all, every Christian person would say that God is indeed Lord of their life. And Saul, prior to being knocked off his high horse, would have declared Jehovah to be Lord of all. But at that point Saul was still not connected to God as he should be.

After he changed his name to Paul, he repeatedly used an interesting term for believers. He referred to us as those who belong to Christ. In Galatians 5:24, for example, he says that "Those who belong to Christ Jesus have crucified the flesh with its passions and desires". One of the passions to which he refers is his own historical driver: ambition.

God is not only Lord, He is also Father. We are part of His household, we belong to Him—being loved as a child and given the responsibility of an heir. We are His, heart, soul and body.

Our derailing moments, where Christ seems to gently turn our head to gaze directly into His eyes, remind us of whose we are. He is helping us to refocus on the reality that we belong to Christ.

Saul's re-naming to Paul was a result of such a refocus. He once saw himself as upward and mobile, scaling the ladder to be something great. But once he saw clearly, it was to change his self-perspective. Paul means *little one*. As he crouched in the corner of Ananias's house in Damascus, blind for three days, he ironically began to see clearly for the first time.

His ambitions changed, later articulated clearly in Philippians 3. He longed only to know Christ, he said, and share in His sufferings. He set his heart to know the power of Christ and share in His resurrection.

You will probably never experience such a derailing event as being stopped on a road and blinded. My guess is that you won't need to. Having the desire to read this material is evidence of that. You want to know the how and why of calling.

As such, you could actually look at Paul's transformed heart and adopt the same priority he did in losing selfish ambition. Before he spelled out the new goals he had taken up in Philippians 3, he outlined what he had needed to leave behind. He talked in terms of placing no confidence in the flesh and actually setting aside that which was previously thought to be a benefit. In our language, Paul was conveying a simple thought, "I need to remember that I bring nothing of worth to the table".

Was he saying that God had mistakenly given him skills and passion? Not at all. God doesn't create us so unique and useful merely to put that aside. In fact, God used those skills powerfully after Paul was on the right set of rails. Paul was saying that his resume of righteousness was not a replacement for Christ, and that an absence of Christ rendered everything else fruitless.

You can apply the same logic.

Think of how you are investing your life. You belong to Christ. Is your heart centred there and your focus on Him? Nothing will quite be as it should unless you have first things first.

Pray:

Lord, I open up my hopes and dreams to you. Will you show me what matters to you, and how I can align my life with yours?

Amen.

Your response:

How much influence has Christ had in the things that have motivated your ambitions and dreams?

_____

_____

_____

… 2.3

Abiding

> Only by dwelling deeply and continually with
> God do we bear kingdom fruit that lasts.

READ FIRST: JOHN 15:1–11

Humans love progress. We like to go forward into the new and the better; to stretch the boundaries of achievement ever further.

God wove that desire into us, and in its right place it is a source of deep joy. But its right place is only found next to Christ. The branch only bears fruit when connected to the vine.

Disconnection brings dysfunction. The works might continue but the fruitfulness ceases.

Consider the sobering example of Moses from Numbers 20. The people had come to him grumbling, as they had done routinely for years. They wanted water and were questioning the strategy of both God and Moses. God commanded Moses to speak to the nearby rock and it would in turn release the needed water.

Moses, however, had been here before. In Exodus 17 he had faced a similar situation. At that time God had told Moses to strike the rock to activate the miracle, and he complied. But this time Moses, now older and probably more tired of the complaints, simply did what he had done the first time, striking the rock instead of speaking to it. God's rebuke of Moses soon followed and he was barred from completing the mission of the Exodus.

Moses had over-reached. He had taken initiative in an area where God insisted on none. He tried making fruit without abiding in the vine.

His successor was to be Joshua. As a young man, Joshua had grown up close enough to Moses to see the value of sticking close to God. When Moses would go into the tent of meeting, he would listen to God's direction then leave to carry it out.

Joshua was a little different, and it was this difference that may well have qualified Him to finish what Moses started. Look at what it says about him in Exodus 33:11:

> "The LORD would speak to Moses face to face, as one speaks to a friend. Then Moses would return to the camp, but his young aide Joshua son of Nun did not leave the tent".

Joshua remained with God long after the talking was done. He abided. He wasn't there to get instructions, that wasn't his role. Therefore, his developing relationship was not based on function. He was putting down spiritual roots that one day would be able to supply the required fruit.

As you and I develop in Christ, it's a natural desire to engage in serving Him in whichever way possible. We are building and utilising the foundational beliefs and relationship we have formed up to that point. But as we seek to grow further, we are more inclined to simply do more or take on added responsibility. But we don't know how to grow our relationship with God. And so, like Moses, we slowly begin to over-extend our spiritual supply lines of guidance and strength.

Scripture defines the mature, spiritual person as one who is empowered by God's Spirit. In the New Testament language, they are called *pneumatikos* (1 Corinthians 3:1). They are people who abide in Christ and are fueled by that relationship.

Every step of spiritual growth you experience is a step closer to Christ.

It is stepping deeper into who you know—His grace, forgiveness, healing and peace—and growing in your ability to live from His provision. It is also about going wider, discovering and experimenting with new elements to the relationship. His mercies are new every morning and there are always undiscovered facets of Gods' nature to explore.

The biggest wall preventing us from discovering new elements of our walk with God is often the same one that does a great job of protecting evangelical Christendom—our comprehensive theology.

My bookshelf contains row upon row of volumes giving intricate detail and commentary on issues relating to salvation, sin, church and systematic theology. They do an incredible job of defining what we know, what is true and what is false. They protect me from heresy and fill me with insights about creation, fall and redemption.

They can also serve to put God, and me, in a somewhat over-defined box.

That's not what they aim to do, but that is what can happen. All those millions of words are our way of explaining the One who is unlimited and beyond full knowing. We even try to contain what is uncontainable by using words like omniscience and omnipresence.

As one who loves knowledge and understanding, I find the study of these materials fills me with awe at the magnitude of God and His creation, and peace at being able to know about Him to some extent.

But that's just the problem, is it not? I can know about Him and I can even read the book He penned, but still not know the author very well at all. Like a book critic, I can lose myself in the finer points of the text or argue the merits of one section over another. But the critic doesn't have a relationship with the author.

Reading of Him is not meant to equal, or even replace, a relationship with Him. In fact, reading without relationship can just as easily lead to extremism and error.

Jesus said that we are to remain in Him and His words are to remain in us (John 15:7). That tells us that His words to us, found both in scripture and ongoing personal guidance, are indispensable and to be cherished. Those words are found in the context of us lingering with Him.

He follows that statement by a promise that tends to rock the best of us: "... ask whatever you wish, and it will be done for you".

Has that been your experience? Apparently, it is supposed to be normal that anything we ask of God He does! For most of us, that is not quite the case. But, for an increasing number, it is a developing reality.

There is a new generation of believers beginning to rise globally. They have stripped off denominational and cultural boundaries, giving them access to the fellowship and testimony of passionate disciples everywhere. They are people of Spirit as well as truth, being grounded in good theology and practice, but determined to follow the whispers of God situationally. They are also proponents of spiritual desire and passion, seeking the face of God with energy and worship.

And importantly, they are a people of presence and power.

They are taking hold again of the example and promises found in the New Testament, believing what Peter said in Acts 2:39 that "The promise (of the Spirit) is for you and your children and for all who are far off—for all whom the Lord our God will call".

They are seeing miracles, salvations and healings at an ever-increasing rate. And rather than being restricted to a radical fringe, these Christians are just as likely to be "middle ground" evangelicals, attending a Baptist or Anglican church. The emerging generation are not satisfied with a theoretical relationship with God. They expect to experience Him and dedicate their lives to doing so. Like Joshua, they remain in God's presence long after the to-do list is dealt with.

Around 70 years ago, a respected Christian author called AW Tozer wrote a book called *The Pursuit of God*[1]. In it he compared the state of western Christianity to the norms found in scripture. When considering our impact on the world, he said:

> *The world is perishing for lack of the knowledge of God and the Church is famishing for want of His Presence. The instant cure of most of our religious ills would be to enter the Presence in spiritual experience, to become suddenly aware that we are in God and that God is in us.*[1]

All these years later, increasing numbers of disciples continue to respond to that challenge.

I am often asked about how to cultivate a life of growing presence and power in the Spirit. Tozer sums it up well when he said we must "enter the Presence in spiritual experience". This is what is happening now all over the world. And it must, or else our Christian witness will become just another religious theory relegated to intellectual debate, while the morality of the world slides ever lower.

It all begins with us learning how to abide in Christ in more profound ways. We are to go deeper and wider into the immensity of our endless God.

Pray:

Lord, I want to dwell with you a little longer today.

Take me deeper into your thoughts and heart. Take me wider into understanding your ways.

Show me your glory, and I will never be the same.

Amen.

References:

1. AW Tozer, *The Pursuit of God: The Human Thirst for the Divine*, Moody Publishers, Chicago, 2015.

Your response:

How well do you believe you are abiding in Christ in this stage of life? In the seasons where you abide most effectively, what is the fruit of that in your life compared to when you are more distant?

2.4

Changing lenses

*To embrace our next upgrade, we must
change our view of what is possible.*

READ FIRST: MATTHEW 14:22–36

When Jesus walked on the water towards the disciples, two changes were taking place to their spiritual perspective.

Firstly, they saw Jesus in a brand new way. The disciples had no framework for what was before them—a man who doesn't sink! Until Jesus identified Himself, their only explanation was that He was some sort of spirit or ghost.

Secondly, the disciples changed their view on what was possible when we partner with Jesus. For Simon, it changed so quickly that he immediately jumped out of the boat and walked on water too!

This was an exercise in changing lenses. Their view of Gods' ways, and of their own potential in Him, would now change forever.

The previous 24 hours had been a most stretching experience for the disciples. The shocking news of John the Baptist's death had been followed by the unprecedented feeding of the five thousand on the hills of Galilee. Then a night of strenuous rowing concluded in this physics-breaking display of night walking.

Prior to this the disciples probably surmised that they had a handle on what Jesus was about. They had been with Him for two years now and seemed to be getting used to His *modus operandi*. They had recently been sent out to pray for the sick and share the gospel and had just reported back to Jesus on their great successes (Mark 6:30).

It was at that moment that Jesus decided to step things up a notch or two.

It was time for the disciples to go on a fast-tracking upgrade, and the news of John the Baptist's death probably added to Jesus' sense of urgency. He knew that His time was coming. Indeed, in a year or so His window of opportunity with the disciples would end.

There were three elements required if the upgrade was to take place: a change of their view of what was possible; a desire within their hearts to embrace growth; and, finally, a commitment to act on what they learned.

The feeding of the five thousand was the icebreaker for changing their view.

This demonstration of power was not just a solution to a hunger problem; it was meant to alter the way the disciples thought and acted. It was to demonstrate that God does not need to stick to the precedents of the past. Multiplying food was new; it couldn't be found in the scrolls anywhere before this. There was no law or formula for how or why it was done. It was simply an act of God's power directed at a specific situation. It was meant to open the disciples' eyes so they might investigate new methods for God to invade our world.

The disciples, however, seemed to miss this point.

Mark's gospel records the same event. But Mark inserts a key phrase that explains why the disciples weren't yet thinking as they should when they saw Jesus on the water. He says, "They were completely amazed, for they had not understood about the loaves; their hearts were hardened" (Mark 6:51–52).

The miracle of the loaves was meant to change their thinking. And it is the same for you and me. Think for a moment of something amazing Jesus has done in your life that was obviously a miracle. Did that event raise the level of your faith or the boundaries of what is possible? It was supposed to.

Most of us find ourselves wondering if God would ever do such a thing again, let alone believing that He would do more and greater! And yet this passage shows us that each miracle is supposed to change our thinking and become the new low-water mark for our faith.

The second element required for the upgrade is to harbour a personal desire for growth.

This sort of desire sets us on a quest of expectant discovery. With it, we see opportunities for God to work where we didn't before. Like a child on a treasure hunt, we see our broken world as a huge playing field on which Team Jesus can do their stuff.

Hebrews 11:6 reminds us that God rewards those who earnestly seek Him. In the original Greek language, that phrase combines a harboured desire for God with a commitment to find Him.

To test the disciples' level of desire, Jesus actually continued to water-walk straight past them, prepared to carry on without getting in the boat. If they weren't curious enough to call out, He was going on alone. Mark 6:48 tells us that Jesus was about to pass them when they finally made contact.

I wonder how often there are lessons and experiences awaiting us during the storms of our life, but we don't think to call out to Jesus in this way? In the midst of our trials, He may well be offering us insight into something brand new—an upgrade of faith or understanding. Proverbs 25:2 reminds us that "It is the glory of God to conceal a matter; to search out a matter is the glory of kings".

In this glorious treasure hunt of faith that we are on, God will at times seem to hide the very principle that might unlock the next phase of our growth. We might wonder how we are to find increase in answers to prayer, or discern answers to our complex issues. And God for a time might seem quite silent.

And yet it is this silence that compels us to seek Him more, and to press our hearts in deeper through prayer, fasting and petition. We are, as the Proverb says, "searching out a matter". And it is that very digging for truth that builds our spiritual capacity to steward what we find.

If we were to have a solution or spiritual "formula" handed to us at our initial request, we might have more faith in the formula than in God Himself. We might even become somewhat entitled, expecting instant answers without growing personal faithfulness.

And yet, the faithfulness and perseverance we exercise in seeking out God for His specific wisdom and power forms us as a safe vessel through which that power can be stewarded. A humble and tenacious saint who listens to and obeys God is the one through whom He works best.

Finally, the last element required to receive the spiritual upgrade is a commitment to act.

Simon learned quickly that if Jesus sets the example, and He calls us to emulate Him, then it is time to move! Immediately he jumped from the boat and started walking to Jesus. No doubt the other disciples had to pick their jaws up from the bottom of the boat as they watched a flawed mortal like Simon walking on the waves.

Simon was no more holy or qualified than the rest. He simply took the initiative, and Jesus encouraged it.

Many people choose to stay in the proverbial boat in life. We focus on our lack of faith or qualification and wonder what the secret is to moving forward. Simon gave us the key, however. You just give it a go!

This is so often how growth in calling occurs. We choose to think a little differently about what is possible. We hear Jesus' gentle guidance to try something new. And we step out of the boat to do something like share our faith, pray for the sick or give sacrificially in faith.

Sometimes we get it right first time and celebrate a victory. At other times we stumble in our attempt. That is what obviously happened to Simon after a few incredible steps on the sea. But Jesus' hand was there to grab him when he began to sink. And there would be plenty more opportunities to extend his faith in the future.

Simon's mistake was to look at the waves and wind. In doing so he lost sight of Jesus.

He needed to refocus.

To fulfil all that is possible requires us to keep our eyes and hearts on Him. Our goal is not to be a superstar of faith; it is to pursue Jesus with all our heart, soul and strength. If our eyes are on Him and our ears are hearing His words, then the rest takes care of itself.

Pray:

Lord, give me eyes to see what you are doing, and ears to hear what you are saying.

Reveal to me the things yet unseen, and give me the faith I need to act on what I find.

Amen.

Your response:

Has there been a miracle done in your past where you have seen God act undeniably to alter a situation? What is it? Do you have faith to see that, and greater things, happen in and through you?

_____

_____

_____

_____

_____

_____

_____

2.5

re:FOCUS on Christ

> When we look away from Christ, we become
> practical atheists—believing God can
> provide, but living like He doesn't.

READ FIRST: MARK 8:14–21

The intended upgrade of faith and deeds that Jesus had in mind for the disciples was not going so well.

It had begun with the feeding of the five thousand and was followed by Jesus walking on water. And yet, because they had not grasped the implications of the multiplication of food, they also failed to see the implications of walking on water (Mark 6:52).

Jesus recognised that the steps of growth He was hoping for were too much of a stretch for the twelve, so He rewound the process somewhat.

This time, He fed four thousand. Surely now they would get the message.

Apparently not.

As they got in the boat to leave, the twelve realised they had only brought one loaf of bread with them for lunch. Given recent events, their response to their lack should have been more faith filled. But instead, their focus had quickly drifted off possibilities and back onto problems.

What we focus on determines our subsequent logic.

They looked at the problem: one loaf, twelve disciples, and they didn't like math. If they had looked first to Jesus, they would certainly have seen the opportunity for another miracle. When we focus on a problem, we naturally tend to play that out, looking at the negative ramifications that will result.

Inversely, when we look expectantly for positive possibilities, or even miracles, our faith and deeds look for ways in which that might happen. We pray in faith or we take steps that expect a win. Obviously, this is the perspective Jesus was hoping for from the disciples at this point.

Jesus responded to their mindset by warning them not to let the leaven of the Pharisees and Herod permeate their life. Leaven is yeast. It is mixed into dough and, as heat is applied in the baking process, the leaven causes the loaf to expand. Leaven was also used in biblical times as a symbol for sin. The loaf broken at Passover, for example, had to be unleavened bread, meaning there was no sin to be found in the offering.

In this passage Jesus is calling out the fault that permeated their thinking—a mindset of practical atheism.

Practical atheism refers to the dynamic where a person claims to follow God and to have faith in His provision, and yet acts as if they are on their own.

The Pharisees were the leaders of the religious system of the day. They followed the rule of law and saw righteousness as coming purely from a person's actions. In their worldview, God did not help, and God demanded perfection. There was no expectation of His provision through faith. Their religious leaven was all about disconnection and judgment.

Herod was the puppet king of the Jews, put in place by the Romans. His family were converts to Judaism and he was a believer by title only. Herod has been remembered in history as being relentlessly ambitious and inherently evil. He killed hundreds of people, including his own family, in the name of self-enhancement. By all definitions, the head of Judaism was completely godless. Again, this leaven is one of self-provision as well as disconnection.

Can you see Jesus' point?

He expects that those who follow Him will live expectantly from His provision of grace, not self-reliance. He does not want His followers to be practical atheists who know they are going to heaven but live as if the rest is up to them.

Again, the disciples monumentally missed the point.

They were at the other end of the boat, still focused on the problem at hand, assuming Jesus was angry at the lack of food. Jesus' advice should have incited transformed thinking, but instead they interpreted it as a rebuke of their poor performance. "Jesus is angry at us now ... it's your fault Peter ... it's always your fault."

In an attempt to save the situation and shake the disciples into clarity, Jesus exclaims, "Why are you talking about the lack of bread?!" In other words, "Why does your logic begin with what you do not have, instead of what can be?"

He then reminded them of the last two miracles He did when bread supplies were low.

You can imagine them trying to figure out that math ... "Let's see ... five loaves, 5000 people, and *twelve* baskets left over. And then seven loaves, 4000 people, with *seven* baskets left over. What is the common ratio in there Matthew? C'mon, you're good with numbers!"

Jesus, head in hand, responded, "Do you still not understand?"

They were looking for a formula where there was none. That's what practical atheism does. It looks for answers in anything but a dynamic, interactive and ongoing relationship with God. There was no formula, just faith. Faith that God gives specific grace to each situation. Faith that He wants to do something amazing. Faith that it is not up to me to have the right amount of bread!

For the Pharisees, the formula involved works done in human strength. But they were never enough! For Herod, it was ambition achieved by human cunning and methods.

Jesus wanted His disciples to focus on Him. If they would fix their eyes on Him, they would remember that it is He who makes anything possible.

> Jesus' next question intentionally shows us how to do just that: "Do you have eyes but fail to see, and ears but fail to hear? And don't you remember?" (Mark 8:18)

Jesus knows our focus can easily drift. For us, even more than the twelve who could literally see Him daily, we need help to keep Jesus at the centre of our thinking and logic.

He first addresses our sight. Jesus expects us to be looking and digesting what we see Him doing at any moment. When we are in a crowd of people, we can be looking with His eyes, expecting to meet needs and bring salvation. Or, we might observe God at work in someone's life through their situation or need. Or, we might be prompted within a conversation to bring encouragement, blessing or an invitation to know God more.

This was Jesus' primary method of ministry. He was constantly surrounded by human need and suffering, and yet He focused on what He knew God was doing at that time. He would later say, "I only do what I see the Father doing" (John 5:19). It was a life of constant interaction with God and facilitation of His will.

This is a skill that takes time to develop, a lifetime in fact. But that practice should start now with us, just as it was expected of the disciples.

Next, Jesus talks about our hearing. If we are unable to see what He is doing, we can listen to His ongoing guidance. He wants our ears to *actually* hear. He declared in John 10:27 that His sheep hear His voice and follow. Again, this takes time and practice, but it is astonishing how often we can perceive God's voice on a daily basis if we focus on listening.

Finally, Jesus says we should remember. The disciples had almost immediately forgotten what Jesus had now done twice when confronted with a lack of supply. If we cannot see what He is doing or hear what He is saying, we have permission to base our logic on what He has previously done.

This is the power of hearing and remembering testimony. When we see an example of God's incredible work and listen to how it came about, it builds faith in us that God could do it again. And Jesus is clearly endorsing that! They had seen the previous multiplication of the loaves and fishes and were now expected to have their faith start at that point.

I have witnessed on many occasions a powerful testimony of healing or salvation and seen the response of God's people in faith and prayer ... and that same miracle happens again in their midst!

What we focus on determines our subsequent logic.

We're not to focus on a formula which we believe God always works to; we are to focus on Him. It is Him we must know, and Him we must seek.

We must continually refocus on Jesus. That relationship is our daily bread, and there is always enough.

Pray:

Lord, open my eyes, my ears and my memory!

Let me see you more clearly, and cooperate with what you are doing.

May I hear your voice, and follow your lead.

May I remember your amazing works, and believe for them again.

Amen!

Your response:

What possibilities exist for a challenge you currently face? What can you see Jesus doing there? What is He saying about it? Can you remember what He has done for you before that He can do again?

_____

_____

_____

2.6

Living from Christ

As we build our faith through intimacy, we can't help but do extraordinary deeds.

READ FIRST: JOHN 21

John chapter 21 is perhaps the clearest passage of scripture for demonstrating the relationship between our specific calling and our communion with Christ.

Since the day three years earlier when Jesus first said "Follow me", Simon Peter had always been totally committed. Recently, however, his commitment *to* Christ had outstripped the strength of his communion *with* Christ.

He had over-promised and under-delivered. Just days earlier, caught up in a frenzy of zeal, he had blurted out, "Even if all fall away, I will not" (Mark 14:29).

Jesus wasn't surprised by Simon's subsequent failure to deliver, in fact, He predicted it. "Three times you will disown me this night." And whilst the others later ran for cover, Simon stayed long enough to fulfil the prophecy. None of the disciples came out looking brave that night, but Simon's was by far the most public scene.

It had been a demoralising failure for Simon. And the incident lingered, hanging in the air, waiting for Jesus to address it. Would He rebuke Simon, retrain him, or maybe even relegate him to the bench until he could control his ego?

Surprisingly, it was to be about none of that.

The scene is a deliberate echo of Jesus' original call to Simon. There was the lake, the boat and the empty nets that became filled with fish. None of this was lost on the disciples. Like the first encounter, this was going to be a conversation about life-calling. And, as in the original call, this one would be defined by the same two words, "Follow me".

God's calling is not cancelled when we fail.

Some days that is easier to believe than others. Romans 11:29 makes clear, however, that God's gifts and His call are irrevocable—He does not take them back. Remember, though, that our calling is not primarily about what we do but about who we are called to be.

If we fail morally, perform badly or abdicate our responsibilities to such an extent that our current position becomes untenable, then that does not equate to a loss of calling. It is just the cancelling of an assignment. Certainly, we may have to make restitution, regain credibility, change context or revise our expectations of life. But God does not stop the work He commenced when He wove us together at conception.

Simon, whose name meant *wispy reed*, was always going to become Peter, the *solid rock*. Jesus had declared it and He was committed to seeing it through.

"Follow me" was a loaded term in their 1st-century Hebrew context. It was how a rabbi invited a prospective disciple to become like them. They were not to just learn information or do certain tasks; they were to become a replica of the rabbi in every way. Cross-reference that idea with Jesus' invitation in Matthew 11:29 from the Message translation:

> *"Walk with me and work with me—watch how I do it. Learn the unforced rhythms of grace".*

This is what it meant to follow Jesus. The rhythms of grace He demonstrated included both walking and working. There was a time to extend and a time to retreat. In the situation we are considering, Simon had over-extended himself, and failed in the process. But, for Jesus, this presented a powerful teaching moment in which to show the disciples how to get their rhythm back.

Simon's ability to extend was only going to be as strong as his ability to retreat back into Jesus. His deeds had outstripped his faith. The problem wasn't that he extended himself; it was that he was doing it out of good intentions alone, not the strength Jesus could give him.

Three times Simon was asked about his capacity to love. Firstly, because Simon had singled himself out as the one who would never desert Jesus. But secondly, because it was love that would enable Simon to feed Jesus' sheep. When Simon had ran out of bravado in the courtyard prior to the rooster crowing, it was because his love for Jesus had lost its effect. The awareness of personal danger was greater at that moment than the awareness of love.

Years later, John would flesh this relationship between fear and love out further, saying:

> *"We know and rely on the love God has for us ... There is no fear in love. But perfect love drives out fear, because fear has to do with punishment. The one who fears is not made perfect in love. We love because he first loved us".* (1 John 4:16, 18–19)

The outworking of our calling, like Simon's, is to love people. But we can only give love to the degree in which we receive love. We cannot give what we do not have.

As they were eating fish on the beach, Jesus was inviting Simon to retreat into the posture of a much-loved son. He was to remember, and be fueled, from love. There would be plenty of time and opportunity for Simon to take on the posture of an heir once more. Jesus even hinted at what was before him, outlining an end to Simon's life that would require huge faith.

But not today. This meeting was all about restitution and recalibration. He was to focus on living from Jesus, not for Him.

But how do you actually live from Christ?

How do you let perfect love so invade your soul that fear is driven out?

How do you reach out in confidence to a lame man, saying, "Such as I have I give to you, rise up and walk"?

How do you prevent the power of your ministry from being limited to the capacity of your own strength?

You do it by intentionally activating the rhythm of grace we call *Faith* and *Deeds*.

The faith element is that of resting as God's child. We rely on Him, not ourselves. We embrace His forgiveness, acceptance and restorative power to build and fuel our soul.

Think of it as digging a deep well and filling it with God's abundant reserves from which we later draw. We are responsible to dig that well ourselves with the small strength we have, in faith that God Himself will fill it.

We dig that well by investing chunks of valuable time in God's presence. We shut the world out, and press in to thoughts of God's ways and ruminate on His word. We look from His view, heaven's reality, at our world. We ask what His will might be and what He wants us to be involved in. We ask for His strength and then rely on the fact that we have it. We ask for more wisdom and thank Him that He provides.

But then, we will be compelled to move out from that place and do something. But not just anything; we do what is impossible in our own strength ... we carry out deeds of faith. What we are, in fact, doing is drawing on that well. We offer to pray for people; we give generously knowing God supplies our need; we show grace in the face of anger and fear. We take a small step of obedience, relying on God to intervene to fulfil His will.

The disciples had in the past been taught this. In Mark 9 we read the account of a man bringing his demon-possessed son for deliverance. Unfortunately, the disciples were lacking in the power required for the job.

Jesus diagnosed their situation as a faith problem. His suggested remedy was for the disciples to fast and pray before they attempted a deed requiring high levels of faith such as this.

And yet, we note Jesus hadn't prayed or fasted immediately before He duly freed the boy from possession. That is because Jesus had for years structured His life around ensuring a deep well of God's presence was always there. Jesus was never over-extended because He consistently took time out to be God's Son. He would wake early to pray, and He would remove Himself from the crowds so He could walk with His Father.

Fasting and praying wasn't some magical formula that somehow obligated God to remove demons. It was a lifestyle strategy that would build that deep spiritual well within. From that they could draw faith, guidance and strength.

By investing time in faith and deeds, we can deepen the well within in ever-increasing measure. And, as a result, have a life that looks more and more like the norms of scripture.

Like Simon, you are called to a life of both faith and deeds. All that matters, however, is your answer to Jesus' question: "Do you love me?"

Pray:

Lord, grant me the faith to stop and rest in you.

Show me more about how to live from you, rather than just for you.

Amen.

Your response:

How well are you doing at creating that deep well of faith and love you need to live all that Christ has for you? What has helped and hindered you doing that?

_____

_____

Group Session 3

RE:FOCUS ON GOD:

This week of readings (2.1 through 2.6) focused on rediscovering the most basic element and motivator of Christian endeavor, our intimacy with God.

Q. What was your overall response to this week of readings?

_____

_____

Now, discuss together your responses from this week's teaching:

2.1 FIRST

*Our commitment to serve God should not
outstrip our communion with God.*

Q. What phrases would you use to describe your first love for Christ in terms of your relationship, worship and responses to Him when you first came to Christ?

2.2 Getting derailed

The two best questions to ask regarding our life's
calling are: "Who am I?" And "Whose am I?"

Q. How much influence has Christ had in the things that have motivated your ambitions and dreams?

2.3 Abiding

Only by dwelling deeply and continually with
God do we bear kingdom fruit that lasts.

Q. How well do you believe you are abiding in Christ in this stage of life? In the seasons where you abide most effectively, what is the fruit of that in your life compared to when you are more distant?

2.4 Changing lenses

To embrace our next upgrade, we must
change our view of what is possible.

Q. Has there been a miracle done in your past where you have seen God act undeniably to alter a situation? What is it? Do you have faith to see that, and greater things, happen in and through you?

2.5 re:FOCUS on Christ

When we look away from Christ, we become practical atheists—believing God can provide, but living like he doesn't.

Q. What possibilities exist for a challenge you currently face? What can you see Jesus doing there? What is He saying about it? Can you remember what He has done for you before that He can do again?

2.6 Living from Christ

As we build our faith through intimacy, we can't help but do extraordinary deeds.

Q. How well are you doing at creating that deep well of faith and love you need to live all that Christ has for you? What has helped and hindered you doing that?

Conclusion of the group meeting

In closing, pray for each other that Christ would give new depth to spiritual intimacy for each participant. Pray that each person would be able to refocus on the presence of God each day, relying on Him for peace and potency to live.

Week 3

re:FOCUS on Character

You are called to become someone unique. God is forming you to be the fulfilment of His calling.

3.1

I have made you

Calling is less about what you achieve,
and more about who you become.

READ FIRST: GENESIS 17:1–17:5

Abraham had long been focused on what he thought was the realisation of his calling: the birth of a son.

God declared that the calling was already in play, the embodiment being Abraham himself. "I have made you a father of many nations", God said (Genesis 17:5).

Abraham was focused on creating a son. God was focused on creating a father of faith.

It was Abraham who needed to refocus.

We live in a performance-oriented culture. The best are rewarded, the wealthiest are respected and the most beautiful are envied. Within that world we have become expert and precise at measuring progress in almost every arena. Whether it be health, fitness, net worth, career, Instagram followers or re-tweets, we have also come to believe that the next level up will bring greater satisfaction.

It is called destination disease, and Abraham felt it too.

He just wanted to get across his own finish line before he died! For him, that line was all about lineage—he absolutely had to have a son. In his time and culture, all that mattered was family heritage. A man's legacy and meaning were lost if he could not pass on his name to another generation.

Worse than that, his own father had called him Abram, a name that literally meant "blessed father of a household". It was almost impossible for him to focus on anything but having a child.

God needed Abram to refocus and He didn't seem to mind if it took some time. It did—24 years in fact. It took that long before Abram took his eyes off arriving at a destination and on to God. What he hadn't noticed along the way was that God had actually made him a father of faith—which was what God had planned all along.

Creating babies is easy for God, building faith is harder.

Faith was a brand-new concept back then. There was no precedent to observe in any other religion—they were all about idol worship and bloody sacrifice. It had never occurred to Abram that this God, who seemed to be speaking to him alone, was uniquely impressed by belief and trust.

Maybe that explains why it was a 24-year-long lesson. There were no examples or scriptures to guide Abram.

And so, God had to teach him the hard way—through character development. God had to take him from being Abram to Abraham. From being the father of a household to becoming the father of nations. He had to demonstrate that calling is less about what you achieve, and more about who you become.

Your name back then was meant to define who you were—your substance, your character. Therefore, if God was to achieve His outcome for this man, then a name change was on the cards.

God was to prove that calling was not about the destination. In fact, He renamed Abram to Abraham even before there was a legitimate son. Abraham's heritage was to flow from who he was: a person of faith. And that faith would be passed on for thousands of years, to the point where even you and I are considered Abraham's children.

> "So also Abraham 'believed God, and it was credited to him as righteousness'. Understand, then, that those who have faith are children of Abraham." (Galatians 3:6–7)

Your unique destiny is defined by the substance of your character, not by your achievements.

Spiritual gifts matter. Skills and opportunities matter too. But you can't function above the level of your character over the long term. Occasionally, you will see some rising star or charismatic genius come into the spotlight. They might appear to be an overnight success, sending a message that only the elite or privileged can rise to any significance.

But history paints us a consistently different picture. At some point the pressure, or the opposition, or the temptation to compromise will conspire to have each one of us fall back to the level of our character.

Character determines consistency. Talk to any "overnight success" and they will tell you their story of a lifetime of discipline, growth and endurance. It's just that they were noticed overnight. Our base level of achievement in all things, be it relationships, career, finance or Christian service, will be the level to which our heart can endure.

God has called you to become someone unique, and a person of depth.

The world will try to define you by all the performance indicators it can create. But God defines you by who you are. It is what happens in our private inner world that determines the state of our outer, observable world.

You may have noticed that most of God's dealings in your life will relate to what happens in your heart. Most of our prayers are about what happens in our world. But God wants to bring focus to things like unforgiveness, shame, pride, fear and resisting temptation. He wants to see you overcome these issues because they are holding you back.

As our heart and capacity grow, the doors of opportunity that we seek can't help but open.

Opposition stands aside when faced with the weighty substance of character. Promotion seeks out the person with proven dedication and enthusiasm. God Himself elevates the one who is faithful to cultivate private morality and intentional humility.

Calling is more about the way you walk than where you are walking to.

When our focus is on where we want to be, the ends can too easily justify the means. Compromise becomes acceptable. People become expendable. It also means that we haven't fulfilled our calling until we have arrived at some destination.

What matters, however, is how we take the journey we are on. Whether we are in fair season or foul, under pressure or in rest, suffering hardship or enjoying breakthrough, we are able to live fully within God's will for us at any moment.

Abraham received his new name before he was a physical father because God had made him fatherly. "I have made you the father of many nations"—a statement of capacity, not accomplishment.

Note that God said, "I have made you". When God wants something done, He makes a person.

The formation process includes the seeds of potential we are born with, but we aren't conceived with the capacity, character and skills we need to become all that God has in mind. We must learn to trust God and to persevere so our hearts become strong. We must experience and overcome disappointments of all kinds, some of which may even incite us to question the goodness and potency of God Himself.

As with Abraham, God is making us a person of faith.

Faith is more than believing God will make everything right, or that nothing goes wrong. God never promised that. In fact, Jesus was pretty clear that trials and disappointments were to be expected. What He promised was the ability for each of us to overcome if we stick close to Him (John 16:33).

Childish faith places an expectation on God to do something for us. Childlike faith has an expectancy that God is good and always more than enough for me in every circumstance. It is childlike faith that Jesus is looking for in His followers.

In 1st John 4:16 the author declares that, "We know and rely on the love God has for us. God is love". We don't have faith in what will happen; we have faith in our perfect God.

Can you see the parallel?

We have faith in God as *someone* we know and can relate to, not an outcome. And when God has a destiny in mind, it is a *someone* He forms, not a destination.

As such, God is not the only one involved. In forming Abraham, He needed Abram to cooperate!

It was not like the man was just a pawn in a cosmic chess game, whose fate was determined without his personal choice. A huge part of the formation process required Abram to be faithful in order to build faith.

The irony is that even though God had fulfilled His mission in making a man of faith, Abraham still clung fiercely to his line in the sand ... a son. When God declared His promises over Abraham's life in Genesis 17, He never mentioned that faith had been His real priority. That moment would come years later, on a hill with Isaac.

It is possible, and way too frequent, for us to lose focus on the things God is doing in our life. Our obsession with the end-game takes our eyes of the now-game.

Do you have destination disease?

God has been forming you into the person He is determined you will be. Is it possible you have taken your focus off what He is doing, in the hope of what He will do?

Pray:

Lord, who are you forming me to be within?

Help me to focus on what you are doing in me, so I can cooperate and grow.

Take my eyes off tomorrow, and fix them on you today.

Amen.

Your response:

Is there a goal or outcome to life that you spend a lot of time thinking about and planning for? Why might your eyes be so fixed on that destination?

_____
_____
_____
_____
_____
_____
_____
_____
_____
_____
_____
_____

3.2

Stuck in a moment

Our next step of guidance may well depend on our obedience to the previous one.

READ FIRST: GENESIS 11:26–12:7

Through the early years of his walk with God, Abram was called yet remained stalled. His destiny lay elusively out of reach and didn't seem to be getting any closer.

Do you know that feeling? You have had the promise of calling but the practice has eluded you.

Abram had settled in a place called Haran with his father and nephew Lot. He was supposed to be far from there in Canaan and without his relatives to influence him.

When God earlier had revealed Himself to Abram, His promise and directions were clear. He was to leave his family and head south-west to Canaan. But west was as far as he got.

Until he obeyed the full direction he was given, Abram would remain stuck between his old life and the blessings of the new. Gods' ways in this regard have not changed. Each of us who seeks to live in the destiny He has for us needs to learn from what happened to Abram.

You may already know what it feels like to be stuck in a moment as Abram was. It is that sense of being torn between potential realities. You may only have a fuzzy idea of the future and so you cannot be too sure how things will really pan out. Did God's promise mean what you took it to mean? Will it be soon, or much later? Would God really call you to such a radical change of life?

And then you look at what you currently have and what you know. It is real, and now. You know these people and how to get by in that culture. You have responsibilities here, with young and old depending on you. And so, movement becomes complicated.

The other issue we grapple with is one of trust. If we do what we sense God requires, will He be true to His side of the bargain? Abram didn't really know God too well at that stage. There were no scriptures to reveal His ways, no historical story for Abram to remember. He had just been spoken to by a deity of which he had no knowledge. In Abram's day, it was normal to worship many deities.

Starting from this unstable place, Abram would grow to become our iconic father of faith.

Like most of us, he eventually headed in the right direction after a somewhat shaky start. He had waited until his father passed away rather than leave him in Haran, a place whose name means *parched land*. It would indeed have been a dry place for Abram. There was no further word from God, no change, and no encouragement from his family.

Abram's character was not yet equal to his calling. There would be no more guidance until He was faithful with what he had.

When we become aware of our stuck-ness, the first area we should refocus is our dedication to obey God. Seldom will He open the next step in our path until we have been obedient in the last. We must invest fully into what we know and where we are, until He makes a way in to something new.

Abram had to leave his father's house, and so do we. Perhaps not literally, but in a spiritual sense there are many elements of our natural life that must be cut off if we are to be free.

Abram's family were idol worshippers. In fact, Haran was the epicenter of worship to the moon god ironically called *Sin*. The whole economy and culture of the city was designed to facilitate a demonically inspired religion. Abram had to choose: would he partake in this agenda, or be separate? We face that same choice in regard to modern-day idols.

Haran was also a place of historical pain for Abram's family. He once had a brother of the same name who had died, no doubt leaving the family mourning for some time.

When they arrived in Haran from Ur, they had stopped there, no doubt remembering their lost son and brother. And so they stayed in that place of dryness and pain, unable to move on. Perhaps they had a sense of obligation to honour Haran by staying. Or their regret may have been enough to lock them too tightly to their past.

Our history makes up a huge part of who we are. And yet, it should be given very little say in who we are to become. We are to adopt the very best of what our heritage grants us. But the best way to honour the past is to build the future.

By leaving his father's house, Abram would have permission to forge a new definition of who he was. Terah had named Abram, essentially boxing him in to become the head of his family. From birth he was expected to carry on its traditions, build its inheritances and live as his ancestors had.

Those closest to us can inadvertently over-define us. They know who we have been, and they know where we have failed. They have lived with our limitations and might find it hard to imagine us without them.

But then God takes hold of our life and, like Abram, we receive a new definition and new promise. No longer are we obligated to our past but are compelled to fulfil a grander future. And so, in the sense of personal definition, we must leave our father's house.

Abram remained stuck in a moment until he had loosened himself from his country, his kindred and his worldly alliances. It took him some time—more than you or I would like to experience—but he got there in the end.

Once his father died, Abram did get out of Haran, but Haran didn't immediately get out of him.

He took Lot with him. And with Lot came the old idol worship and family baggage. It was an awkward tension for them both, and the land was not able to support their combined presence. So eventually, Abram suggested they separate, letting Lot choose his preferred territory.

Lot took the best for himself, just as the world does. But Abram had begun to have faith in God to provide, rather than rely on human cunning. Dismissing Lot was a cutting of the last connection to his past. Abram was free to be God's person, separate from obligation or definition from those who claimed to know him best.

As soon as Lot left, the Lord honoured Abram's choice and revealed Himself again (Genesis 13:14). He confirmed the promises and gave instruction on how to proceed. It is incredible how clear and how frequent the Lord's guidance is when we commit ourselves to His way.

Abram's faith was soon to be tested at a higher level, however, when he was confronted with the temptation to hoard riches. In Genesis 14 we are told that Abram went to war with those who plundered the region which Lot was inhabiting. They had taken Lot as a hostage, but God allowed Abram a great victory against high odds. He didn't just get his nephew back; the riches of the whole region came with him. All Abram had to do was hang on to it and no one would argue his claim.

And yet it was the wealth of corruption. The city of Sodom where Lot had dwelt was evil to the core and to keep its money was to endorse the source. The king of Sodom offered that Abram could bank the cash, but it would have come with long political strings attached. If Abram were to keep the money, he would owe the king a big favour. That was not a favour Abram wanted to keep, and so the money was left behind.

Again, straight after this act of faith-motivated obedience, God revealed Himself powerfully to Abram.

This time, the promises became unconditional. A covenant was made between God and Abram, where the onus was on God to fulfil what had been promised (Genesis 15).

Abram's role was, once again, to simply believe.

Unfortunately, even belief can be tarnished. Abram was now convinced that he would have a son but, with Sarai now barren, he decided God must have had a plan B. Abram produced a child through his maidservant, Hagar, believing that was how it must be achieved.

Silence from God followed.

The Lord was not impressed by the initiative shown by Abram. And now there was also an Ishmael to deal with. And so, between the birth of Ishmael and the ultimate faith-test of sacrificing Isaac, another 28 years of faith building took place. That is potentially 40 years in total from the time Abram was called to leave Ur until he passed that hardest of tests in Genesis 22.

During that time, however, Abram had finally become a man of faith and was ready to work with God on his terms. There had been many ups and downs along the way, and it had taken a long time to get this man unstuck.

How about you? Is there a sense that you just know that the fullness of God's favour is not being seen in your life?

We do not earn God's blessing by being good. We learn to be good stewards of his blessing by being faithful. His supply is without limit and his ability to give us increase has no bounds. He wants to bless. But we must be faithful carriers of that blessing because it is for the good of the world.

We remain stuck until we develop faithful obedience to what we have already been told to do. Scripture gives clear guidelines, and God is able to whisper His will into your spirit.

We need to refocus on character as it is the great qualifier to fulfilling God's plans.

Pray:

Lord, show me if I am stuck in a moment because of things I haven't let go of, or something new I should be doing.

Lord, give me the strength to break free.

Amen.

Your response:

What are the things that conspire to keep you stuck in a moment?

_____

_____

_____

_____

_____

_____

_____

_____

_____

_____

_____

_____

3.3

Growing character

> When all forms of supply are cut off except
> God Himself, we turn to Him more deeply
> and grow like Him more fully.

READ FIRST: LUKE 4:1–22

Even Jesus needed to grow in maturity to fulfil His calling.

Think about that for a moment. He was without fault. How do you possibly improve on that?

It might help to think in terms of quality and quantity. All that Jesus was from the moment of conception was of perfect quality. And yet He was still born an infant, with an infant's capacity. He had to grow in maturity, like the rest of us. The quantity of His character had to grow.

> "Son though he was, he learned obedience from what he suffered and, once made perfect, he became the source of eternal salvation for all who obey him." (Hebrews 5:8–9)

That word translated as *perfect* is the Greek word *teleioo*, which means complete, or mature. Jesus' character needed to reach its fullness before He could complete His ultimate assignment.

That is why Jesus was sent by the Spirit into the wilderness. And why you are occasionally sent there too.

It is a vital part of character development, and character is a major requirement of kingdom work. We aren't to merely do good, powerful or righteous things. We are to be good, powerful and righteous people.

There are a number of elements which contribute to our level of fruitfulness over the long term. Factors such as experience, skill and spiritual gifting all determine the high point we might hope to sustain.

For short periods, any element may provide a way for a particularly impressive outcome to come about. Our skills might develop a new widget or ministry, our experience may solve a difficult problem, and a spiritual gift may bring about a miracle or breakthrough.

The level at which we can sustainably impact the world, however, is determined by the level of our character.

At some point, either through pressure, moral failure, sustained fatigue, relational challenges, or any number of limiting factors, we always fall back to our level of capacity to endure in an ethical way.

The most public example of this in our day has been the plight of many gifted Christian leaders. Their oratory, enthusiasm or particular strategy may have elevated their profile and brought success. But, sadly, we regularly see them fall from grace because of personal weakness or hidden sin. Their gifts outstripped their character, and the fallback was painful. When it happens, it is an incredible loss to the kingdom.

We can relate to this example because it is often such a visible fall. And yet, within churches the same thing happens every week to the general folk who fill our pews. Marriages fail, businesses are lost and ministries break because we try to operate beyond the level of our character.

Thankfully, God has a plan for growing our character. We just need to recognise and cooperate with it!

The wilderness experience that Jesus undertook is a great example of this process.

He was already doing very well. So well that at His baptism God Himself declared audibly that He was well pleased with Jesus. He had an A+ already, but that simply qualified Him for the next upgrade. He had gone as far as He was going to go without some new spiritual training.

And so, full of the Spirit, Jesus headed into the wilderness.

Now, most people view the wilderness as a negative experience. But that is simply not true. In fact, the wilderness is where we do the most growing! It is a time where our walk with God grows more intimate and our priorities are trimmed of worldly excess.

Or perhaps we might replace the word "trimmed" with "pruned".

When we have been proven fruitful, as Jesus had, a character-growing phase can feel exactly like being pruned. We shouldn't be surprised; after all, Jesus used the same expression in John 15:1–2:

> "I am the true vine, and my Father is the gardener. He cuts off every branch in me that bears no fruit, while every branch that does bear fruit he prunes so that it will be even more fruitful".

Pruning essentially means that our previous methods of bearing fruit are trimmed off. You will know you have been pruned when the things you did almost recreationally before, and that produced a great result, are no longer effective.

You may feel like saying, "Hey, what just happened? All the things that I know work, no longer do!" What once came easily now becomes impossible. That which had a momentum of its own now seems to have stalled, and can't be restarted.

At this point, many of us determine to dig deep and push through. But we find ourselves becoming rapidly exhausted. All worldly sources of supply seem cut off. It feels like a spiritual desert!

But, a desert is a place where there is no supply. A wilderness is different. In the wilderness there is still a wealth of supply; it is just that it's not from the infrastructure that the world provides. There are streams and shelter and life all around. But all of these are provided by God Himself, not humanity.

It may sound strange, but in our periods of peak fruitfulness we can fail to consider that it is not just God who is at work. Sure, He is doing His vital part, but other factors come alongside, which give added impetus. The resources, people, training and other mechanisms of support all add to the momentum. This is good and is a natural part of how we partner with God and each other to make progress.

But the wilderness cuts off all forms of supply other than God Himself. And that can feel strange!

At that point, a wilderness can turn into a desert if we don't quickly turn to God and grow our intimacy with Him. When Jesus entered His wilderness, He commenced a new phase of prayer and fasting. He knew that the trials coming His way were at a whole new level, and He therefore committed to digging a much deeper well of the Father's presence in His life.

When we don't understand this principle, we tend to react somewhat differently. We will find ourselves asking, "What did I do wrong?" or, "Whose fault is this?" or, "Where did you go, God?"

It is not about blame, failure or abandonment. It is about you getting an upgrade.

We need to observe and embrace the tide of God's work ebbing and flowing in our lives. Rather than fight His ways, we should remember Jesus' words from Matthew 11:29 (MSG), "Walk with me and work with me—watch how I do it. Learn the unforced rhythms of grace".

This rhythm of grace that builds our character requires the same advance and retreat cycle that we have discussed previously. If we learn to watch what He is doing, then we won't wear out or break down.

Before Jesus could push through to a new level of working with God, He had to pull back.

The wilderness season is our moment to pull back. It can last for a moment, or for years, depending on the situation and calling upon our lives.

After the wilderness, we can begin to push through to new places. In this phase of advance, we grow perseverance and hope through our tenacity, born of our time in retreat.

This rhythm of grace works into us new levels of dependency on God. We replace hubris with humility. Our cries for rescue turn into cries for transformation. Ultimately, it is about growing our internal world so that our external world can be different.

Your calling is all about character.

Pray:

Lord, what season am I in now?

Am I to press forward or pull back?

Either way, help me to remain in you as my source of supply.

Amen.

Your response:

Have you ever been pruned? How did that come about, and what was the long-term result?

_____

_____

_____

3.4

The fruit of perseverance

*From our worst of circumstance God
plans to bring the fruit of hope.*

READ FIRST: JAMES 1:2–4

There are seasons where we feel trapped, with nowhere to turn.

We may be in a job that turned out to be a bad fit. We are far from our sweet-spot and aren't getting sympathy or support. But we can't just quit—we have obligations, and bills to pay—we are stuck there.

Or, we might find ourselves embedded in relationships that have turned toxic and accusatory. People think badly of us and we feel disempowered to speak up. We may not be experiencing abuse, but we certainly aren't appreciated either. We are being drained emotionally, day after day. But if we were to leave, it would tear innocent people apart and disappoint those we care about.

Or, perhaps our body is not functioning as it should. We have a disease without a cure and pain that never leaves. Treatment is out of reach, and those who support us are under too much strain.

Maybe you are being vilified for your faith. You have had to make a stand on a moral issue and it is causing backlash.

These are the "trials of many kinds" referred to in James 1:2–4.

God doesn't need to orchestrate the difficulties we find ourselves in; the world is doing a good job of that. But even when life deals us a pair of twos, He can still win the hand. In fact, God is so good at bringing good from evil that you can understand people's mistaken opinion that it was God who instigated it in the first place.

Our trials need not be connected to Christian persecution, although they might be. They are usually just part of being in our broken world. And yet God, in the fullness of His mystery, can and will use these circumstances to bring about a much higher prize than circumstantial release.

That prize is maturity of character. God wants you perfected!

He is constantly looking for opportunities to bring you an upgrade. In doing so, He can make gold from ashes.

"... for a little while you may have had to suffer grief in all kinds of trials. These have come so that the proven genuineness of your faith—of more worth than gold ... may result in praise, glory and honour when Jesus Christ is revealed." (1 Peter 1:6–7)

Trials are our moment to prove the genuineness of faith, a faith developed in the time of pruning and wilderness. That faith produces deeds, the most profound of which are the overcoming of hardships, rather than needing to escape them.

Any trial can be turned to our advantage if we allow it to test our faith in God and develop character (James 1:3). But we need to recognise and participate in the process. This begins by assuming that, whatever difficult season we are in, God wants to and can bring something of immense worth out of it.

This assumption changes our prayer life. Rather than pleading for escape, we begin plotting for victory. Rather than cooperating with depressing logic, we partner with hope.

Have you noticed that we normally ask God for guidance more when things are going bad? You may have found yourself praying, "I'm uncomfortable now God, get me out of here!" or, "It can't possibly be your plan for me to be here. But I can't get out ... heeeelp!"

Where is that same desperation for a change when seas are calm and the skies are blue? And yet, as is so often the case, pruning begins after such seasons of clear-skied fruitfulness.

Thankfully, the Apostle Paul deconstructed the process of using trials to produce the desired outcome in Romans 5:3–4:

> "(We) glory in our sufferings, because we know that suffering produces perseverance; perseverance, character; and character, hope".

Hope, Paul says, is the fruit of developed character. The mature and complete believer looks expectantly to what God can do, rather than dwelling on the long list of things we resent Him not doing. Christian maturity is full of optimism.

In Paul's sequence of character growth, there are three consecutive choices we can make that determine where we end up. They are like forks in the road, and taking the right path is vital.

The first fork occurs when we are confronted with our trial. We look at the imperfect situation before us and must make a choice: do I stay, or do I run? If I stay, the suffering ultimately produces perseverance. If I run, I might escape, but I lose the benefit that God says is worth more than gold.

God values different things to us. We cherish comfort and material reward. God values only what is eternal. Hope, faith and love are the only things we get to take to heaven with us.

> *"For now we see only a reflection as in a mirror; then we shall see face to face. ... And now these three remain: faith, hope and love."* (1 Corinthians 13:12–13)

In the face of difficulty, God calls us to take the higher road and reap an eternal reward. The list of rewards that wait for those who overcome are spelled out through scriptures like Revelation 2 and 3, where Jesus encourages the churches. The gains are worth enduring for and make our temporal difficulty seem insignificant and brief.

The second fork in our path occurs as soon as we have chosen to stick things out. Suffering is supposed to produce perseverance, but that is not always the case. We can choose to persevere, or we can choose to compromise. The latter is a way to mitigate discomfort. It is a commitment to stay in our tough situation but to reduce the pain by giving in to those around us. We might bend our morals to alleviate persecution, or stop speaking up against evil.

Moral compromise is the enemy of character. Like a leaky tap, it lets the pressure escape only to leave a mess on the floor. Nothing is gained since we remain in the situation, leaving us to navigate the shame management of letting ourselves down.

Character is formed under pressure. It feels the load and looks to God for strength to resist. In that pressured situation, new grace is found and greater faith experienced for our next season of life. The choice to test our faith is a choice to trust in God to give us exactly the amount of grace needed to overcome any situation. Look at how Paul explains this through his own painful experience:

> "But [God] said to me, 'My grace is sufficient for you, for my power is made perfect in weakness'. Therefore I will boast all the more gladly about my weaknesses, so that Christ's power may rest on me. That is why, for Christ's sake, I delight in weaknesses, in insults, in hardships, in persecutions, in difficulties. For when I am weak, then I am strong". (2 Corinthians 12:9–10)

Grace always meets the need. A choice to persevere is an invitation for God to do what we never could do alone. An invitation He always accepts.

The final fork in the road comes to the one who perseveres. Even after enduring so much, it is possible to veer off course and lose the promised benefit. Perseverance is meant to produce hope, and does so for those who adopt an expectant spirit.

However, we can choose a lesser path, that of disappointment.

Having experienced hardship and pain, we can assume that all of life is like that. We begin to live in perpetual expectation of sadness, and expect God to always expose us to disappointment. We begin to believe that joy is for other people and that faith is a naive trait of the simple minded.

After all, our world is broken and hardship is always coming, right?

Possibly, yes! But hope is not based on what is circumstantial but on what is substantial; that is, Christ in us, the hope of glory (Colossians 1:27). God undergirds and supports us through every situation so that we cannot fail.

Hope expects the best while overcoming the worst.

At those times when we feel hemmed in by our trials, we are in fact in the confines of the greatest arena of the cosmos. God looks on, with the saints of old, cheering our faithfulness. Suffering should not incite us to change course, but should incite our determination to fulfil our calling in God's strength.

> *"Therefore, since we are surrounded by such a great cloud of witnesses ... let us run with perseverance the race marked out for us."* (Hebrews 12:1)

Pray:

Lord, thank you for the strength you give me to overcome through any trial.

Your grace is always enough. Help me to embrace that grace today.

Amen.

Your response:

In recent times, have you been able to let suffering do its work in you to produce character and hope? What was your situation, and how did you respond?

_____

_____

_____

_____

_____

_____

_____

_____

3.5

The wilderness effect

Our wilderness is designed to draw us to God—lest we find ourselves in a desert.

READ FIRST: HOSEA 2:14–16

When Jesus was led by the Spirit into the wilderness, it was part of God's design for Him. He experienced the type of wilderness journey described by Hosea, where God meets us and makes us more fruitful.

This type of strategic retreat is the part of God's rhythm where we intentionally pull back, rather than push forward in perseverance. We lean in to Him in a new and deeper way, and our faith matures as a result.

The wilderness is part of God's plan for all of us. It is not meant to be negative in any way, although it can certainly be painted that way. Even in scripture, we see accounts of those who entered such a season, for whom it did not end well.

For some, the season seemed to last an incredibly long time. Moses needed 40 years; David and Joseph took 14 years; the Apostle Paul, too, spent around 14 years in obscurity as God disassembled his pride. It needn't last that long, however. As we have seen, Jesus stepped into His upgrade in 40 days.

What that tells us is that our wilderness seasons take as long as they must to get the required transformation in place. It also shows us that we can choose to cooperate or we can mishandle the season completely, possibly lengthening its duration.

In an extreme case, such as that of the Israelite nation of the Exodus, it is possible to disqualify ourselves completely. God had called the entire nation into the wilderness to worship and yet all but two perished. We are told in 1 Corinthians 10:11 that these things were recorded for us as warnings so that we might not emulate their example. Indeed, this should be incredibly sobering for all of us.

The scriptural accounts prove to us that our participation in the season determines the experience and outcome. We can do it the easy way or the hard way, but we are not coming out until God has had His way!

Jesus engaged in the wilderness voluntarily, and by design. He knew it was God's plan: that He would meet Him more deeply there and that He would grow. As such, it was a stretching and yet positive experience.

Moses, on the other hand, went in to his wilderness by default, rather than God's design. He had killed an Egyptian and was forced to flee. God used that opportunity to make him into one who would deliver the nation in God's way, not man's way.

Abraham went into the wilderness through defiant determination. He simply didn't want to follow God's plan to enter Canaan and chose instead Haran, the parched land. And even after he moved out of that place, it still took 24 years to get the parched land out of him.

Even those who aren't close to God, and yet are His chosen instrument to impact the world, will experience God's growth process. Winston Churchill, for example, was one born into privilege and raised to rule. He had risen to national fame through early military exploits and war correspondence. And yet, through political mishap and strategic error, he found himself in public exile, shunned by his nation between the world wars.

This ten-year phase of Winston's life is famously called the "wilderness years". In his depression he turned to writing the four-volume history of his ancestor General John Churchill, Duke of Marlborough. The general was the pivotal figure in the wars of the early 1700s against Louis XIV of France.

During this soul-searching period for Winston, he began to see that Adolf Hitler was becoming the modern-day version of the power-hungry Louis—someone bent on accumulating territory at any cost. In Marlborough, Winston saw his own template, and subsequently became the sole voice of outcry against inevitable tyranny.

His wilderness became the most pivotal period of Winston's life, preparing him uniquely to seize the reins and save his nation. He would never have chosen his path to success, and yet he and the whole world lived to see the legacy of his character-forming retreat.

The only time a wilderness can fail in its outcome is if we choose to make it a desert. If, rather than digging deeper into the wellspring of God, we choose to go it alone, then we can stay parched and stalled by our own design.

Wilderness periods are frequently marked by a sense of feeling cut off from worldly forms of supply. Whether it be relational networks, income streams, our reputation, long-held skills or conventional resources, it just seems that what brought us fruit yesterday is redundant today.

God is wanting us to press in to Him exclusively, and more deeply. Only then can the source of supply increase in its impact. His goal is to grow our character, to make us bigger on the inside through increased grace.

Our best model to follow through the wilderness is, of course, Jesus. In Luke 4:1–14, we see Him enter the wilderness full of the Spirit but leave in the power of the Spirit. This is a significant, and non-accidental, point for Luke to raise.

Jesus was perfect on the way in, but more complete on the way out.

As we develop in our faith, we too come across these differentiations of maturity. A deeply significant moment occurs when we are able to overcome the power of our flesh and broken past. We transition into someone who is empowered predominantly by God's Spirit. This happens sometime after our salvation experience, as the sanctification process transforms us from being a carnal Christian to a spiritual Christian (1 Corinthians 3:1).

In this state of developing freedom, we become more able to grow in spiritual capacity. Transforming is often a precursor to engaging the world in a more impacting way. Jesus had developed throughout His early life, but now it was time to pull back and take advantage of a wilderness.

His experience highlights the three major transformations that take place as we draw more deeply on God. These are articulated in Jesus' responses from the Old Testament to the temptations the devil dangled before Him.

"Man shall not live by bread alone." (Luke 4:4)

Jesus had been tempted to make bread from a stone. It was a temptation aimed at the human preference that God would alter our circumstances to alleviate discomfort. The wilderness brings to light the cravings we harbour for comfort and easy supply. Prior to our wilderness, worldly supply possibly came easily, and we hadn't developed the ability to wait or look to God as our main source of comfort.

Jesus quoted Deuteronomy 8:3, where God had explained to the Hebrews that their wilderness was aimed at having them hunger for God's word more than for food.

The beauty of the wilderness is that, by withholding supply from our childish cravings, we begin to live from our God of unlimited grace. Our cries for rescue are replaced by cries for transforming relationship.

"Worship the Lord your God and serve Him only." (Luke 4:8)

This next statement is Jesus' response to Satan's offer of the empires of the world. All Jesus had to do was worship the devil. It sounds unthinkable to us, and thankfully Jesus had no interest in the offer. But we can look at the timing of the temptation and learn from it ourselves.

The timing of our wilderness experiences often interrupts an acceleration in the momentum of life. At the time, we might be on a roll—gaining ground and seeing a lot of potential ahead. It is tempting for us at those moments to invest even more heavily in our career or ministry in the hope that it will be our big thing.

We don't notice, however, that we may have been creeping into borrowed time. The hours we should spend with God are given to work. The money we should contribute to the kingdom is spent on the next necessary gadget. We start to serve the empire we are building, often blindly because we are convinced that we are doing God's will, God's way.

In our wilderness, God finds a way to confront the idols we are serving. He says, "Will you pause that mindset long enough to worship me?" or, "Are you willing to let that agenda go altogether?"

We come out of these seasons with our satisfaction found in Him alone. We don't need the success and don't yearn for the next big win.

"Do not put the Lord your God to the test." (Luke 4:12)

In this statement, Jesus was refusing to presume on God's grace to save Him if He were to jump off the temple heights. Some people's faith is built on the assumption that God is obliged to respond to our expectations. We get indignant when things go wrong, and angry when we see injustice everywhere. We expect God to come through on our terms.

But the wilderness converts our hubris to humility.

We no longer pretend to understand His ways. We are satisfied to live in a degree of mystery. We are thankful for all we have, without expecting more continually.

Can you see the common thread in the fruit of our wilderness seasons? Life becomes much less about us and much more about Him.

These seasons are testing, but they are something to be both embraced and cherished. Long or short, the wilderness is a place to restore our hope in God and build our faith.

Pray:

Lord, thank you for the times of retreat. When I go through those seasons, help me to pause and see what you are doing in me. Help me to draw from you in a new way.

Amen.

Your response:

Have you ever been through a season in the spiritual wilderness? What were the signs that it was a wilderness?

_____

_____

_____

_____

_____

_____

_____

3.6

re:FOCUS on character

Destiny is focused on the way we take the journey, never on the outcome.

READ FIRST: GENESIS 16

Most of us have our version of an Ishmael in our story.

It is that decision we make in haste that has unfortunate ramifications for a long time. It may the relationship we should have halted earlier, or the huge debt we should never have signed on for, or the moment of sinful indulgence that resulted in a long string of hurt lives.

It happens when we lose focus. Our earthly desires overrule our rationale. Or, like Abram, we feel obliged to act when God does not. We can't figure out where faith stops and our initiative should begin. It is all a little blurry and unknown.

If we are in the middle of a wilderness season, the tendency to lose focus is amplified. It is that in-between season, between the promise and the reality, that requires even deeper faith if we are to get through.

While we are in transition, the character He is forming is not yet substantive. The inner tension created by unfulfilled desires pulls us sideways. That tension is supposed to draw us to God, that's why He creates it. He is drawing us to become who we are called to be.

A faith journey can be like walking a balance beam. On either side are opposing temptations that draw us in to their error. The result of each is that we disconnect from the vital connection with God that fuels progress.

On one side is the temptation to abdicate responsibility.

Abram knew that he was to have a family one day, even though he was aged. He knew that only God could open Sarai's womb. Therefore, faith at that point could be defined as doing nothing and just waiting to see God work. And yet, Abram still had to be a loving husband for Sarai. This was to be no immaculate conception!

Beyond that, God expected Abram to survey the land and also prepare his heart for what would one day be a nation. And so Abram still had responsibilities; he was expected to be faithful. Mature faith in God does not equate to abdication of responsibility.

One of the most profound aspects of God's maturing process is the evolving of our partnership with Him. For a new believer, faith takes a simpler form—it is about God working for them. Like an infant, we passively wait for God's supply. And so often He does supply! Salvation is received this way. We can do nothing but accept what He has done.

But, as we mature, God draws us into a deeper relationship where we become co-workers. We are treated as sons and heirs. What that looks like is a transition from God working for us to God working progressively more through us.

We can see it at play in the Hebrew Exodus. When they entered their wilderness, they thought like slaves and relied totally on God working for them. Their original "soup and spoon" worldview required them to merely turn up and partake of God's provision.

But that mindset would not work in the Promised Land! They would need to go to war. They needed to hear and cooperate with God's plans. God summarised this big lesson in Deuteronomy 8:2–3, saying:

> "Remember how the LORD your God led you all the way in the wilderness these forty years, to humble and test you in order to know what was in your heart, whether or not you would keep his commands. He humbled you, causing you to hunger and then feeding you with manna, which neither you nor your ancestors had known, to teach you that man does not live on bread alone but on every word that comes from the mouth of the LORD".

They were taught to listen and cooperate. They were to be co-workers, with a defined role to play.

Now, if the error of one side of the balance beam of faith is abdication, the other is self-reliance.

Abram was tired of what felt like inaction. He was feeling the tension of unmet promises, and in that moment Sarai's logic was compelling. "God hadn't brought a child, He must want us to help Him out a different way. Otherwise, He would have done it by now."

Their logic failed to factor in that God's will can only be achieved in God's way. He had planned that Sarai would have the child and no deviation was required. Character is never built through compromise, and the fruits of sin cannot be held up as a replacement for God's plan.

God's plan for Abram had two tiers. One was to build a man of faith; the next was to build a nation from him that would be God's people.

But now there was Ishmael. And, as is so often the case with our bad choices, the result can't just disappear.

Could God not, therefore, redeem the situation and work it all out for good? Could Abram's plan become God's new Plan A? The son was even named Ishmael, which means *God hears*, inferring that Ishmael was God's idea. Indeed, Abram even pleaded this case to God, saying, "If only Ishmael might live under your blessing". God's response is telling:

"Yes, but your wife Sarah will bear you a son, and you will call him Isaac. I will establish my covenant with him as an everlasting covenant for his descendants after him". (Genesis 17:19)

God's "yes" meant that He would work out a plan for Ishmael, but it would never be Isaac's plan. God takes our mistakes and uses them for good, but that does not infer that our mistakes were necessary for God to fulfil his plan. Nor does it mean that our mistakes can become God's plan simply because they can't be brushed aside.

Ishmael was here to stay, and the world continues to be deeply affected by the nations that descended from him. The legacy of our decisions usually stays with us, but God's real Plan A still prevails.

His plan is to build a person of a certain character, such as an Abraham from an Abram. Ishmaels may happen along the way, making our path more cluttered or imperfect than we would like. But God's call is irrevocable (Romans 11:29).

How, then, do we refocus?

If we have gone off track and carry the burden of our mistakes and self-will, how do we get our eyes back on God and His ways? Or, if we have been lazy with our faith, waiting for God to act while we abdicate any responsibility to obey, how do we get back on track?

The first step is always to come back to God personally. We must strip ourselves of religious pretense and self-justification and bow before Him. Abram did this after Ishmael had grown somewhat and before Isaac had been conceived. Abram had spent time learning, waiting and maturing. It was only then that God could say, "I have made you a father of many nations" (Genesis 17:5).

Only God can tell us when and how to wait, and where to act. There is no pre-existing formula to follow blindly—no precedent for your unique situation or calling. You need to simply listen to God and submit to Him.

Whether we are in a phase of pushing through in perseverance, or of pulling back in retreat, it will require us to press in to Him more deeply.

Then, once our engagement with God is clear, we are in a position to actually assess His ways, and to cooperate with what He is doing in us. When we are close to God, we can recognise our inner tension to go off track and focus again on our particular path of faith and deeds.

Perhaps He has called us to do something but we have turned that into self-fueled striving. We must then adopt a Paul-like way of working with God in partnership, where he would "strenuously contend with the energy Christ gives" (Colossians 1:29).

Or perhaps He has called us to rest, but we have turned that into lazy abdication. We must realise that so much of living in Sabbath is to invest in the re-creation of our soul through feeding our inner world.

Moses, at one of his darkest and most frustrated hours, cried out for God to reveal His ways. He could see what God ultimately wanted to be done, but could also see no way for that to happen. He was tired and disillusioned. God's response was, as always, profound: "My Presence will go with you, and I will give you rest". (Exodus 33:14)

This was to be Moses' rhythm of grace. Powerful deeds would be done and perseverance required—but only in partnership with God's Presence. He would also find rest as they journeyed their wilderness as long as they followed His guidance. Without Moses pressing deeply in to God personally, this strategy would never have been found.

I wonder what your situation is, and what unique path will make you into the person God wants. Who is the character you are becoming?

Pray:

Lord, show me your ways that I might partner with what you are doing.

Guide me in your paths, so I might follow you without out-pacing your timing.

Build my character so I might be the person you need me to be.

Amen.

Your response:

What name(s) might encapsulate the identity of who God has been forming you to be throughout your life?

_____

_____

_____

_____

_____

_____

_____

_____

_____

_____

_____

_____

Group Session 4

RE:FOCUS ON CHARACTER:

This week of readings (3.1 through 3.6) focused on becoming the person God has called you to be. What we do will ultimately come from who we are, but are comfortable in our own skin on the journey?

Q. What was your overall response to this week of readings?

_____

_____

Now, discuss together your responses from this week's teaching:

3.1 I HAVE MADE YOU

Calling is less about what you achieve, and more about who you become.

Q. Is there a goal or outcome to life that you spend a lot of time thinking about and planning for? Why might your eyes be so fixed on that destination?

3.2 Stuck in a moment

*Our next step of guidance may well depend
on our obedience to the previous one.*

Q. What are the things that conspire to keep you stuck in a moment?

3.3 Growing character

*When all forms of supply are cut off except God himself, we
turn to him more deeply and grow like him more fully.*

Q. Have you ever been pruned? How did that come about, and what was the long-term result?

3.4 The fruit of perseverance

*From our worst of circumstance,
God plans to bring the fruit of hope.*

Q. In recent times, have you been able to let suffering do its work in you to produce character and hope? What was your situation, and how did you respond?

3.5 The wilderness effect

Our wilderness is designed to draw us to God—
lest we find ourselves in a desert.

Q. Have you ever been through a season in the spiritual wilderness? What were the signs that it was a wilderness?

3.6 re:FOCUS on character

Destiny is focused on the way we take the
journey, never on the outcome.

Q. What name(s) might encapsulate the identity of who God has been forming you to be throughout your life?

Conclusion of the group meeting

In closing, pray for each other that God would reveal more of what He is doing, and who He is forming within each participant.

Week 4

re:FOCUS on People

When you find your people, you have found your purpose. You are called to influence those God has put around you.

4.1

People are your purpose

When you find your people, you
have found your purpose.

READ FIRST: MARK 6:31–37

"Send the people away", the disciples said.

It was a statement that galvanised Jesus' resolve and catalysed one of His most remembered miracles: the feeding of the five thousand.

How often, though, do we share the disciples' sentiments?

People make things messy and unpredictable. They often ruin our plans, alter our schedule and make life complicated. For those who are task oriented, people can even appear to be the problem that stops us fulfilling our purpose!

There is no escaping the raw fact, however: people *are* your purpose. They are not the problem, they are the prize.

People are not part of the asset pool we must assemble to get our goal achieved. People are not a necessary means to an end; they are the end.

Neither are people our projects. We can't determine to save them, or change them into what we think they should be. Those things aren't up to us. God has given them choice and it is He who draws and judges them.

People are the focus of our calling in God. The love He gives is to be directed on them. Preferably as individuals. Look at the way Peter articulated this principle in his later years:

> *"Each of you should use whatever gift you have received to serve others, as faithful stewards of God's grace in its various forms".* (1 Peter 4:10)

Many times I have been asked how a person can grow in the power of the Holy Spirit and in the use of spiritual gifts. The answer is to serve people more. God seems to save His most powerful and creative works for meeting the needs of real people who need grace.

At least as many disciples ask for insights in discerning their specific calling in God. However, I find that question is almost never asked by those who are already deeply invested in people.

When you find your people, you find your purpose.

People and purpose are intrinsically connected. If we follow Paul's analogy from 1 Corinthians 12, we are all parts of one body. Therefore, if I am a hand, I cannot fulfil what I am unless I am connected to the arm!

Your calling in life is not just about you.

Our culture, however, emphasises the opposite view, saying that your purpose is an individualistic pursuit of personal accomplishment. Many sincere Christians, with that worldly principle embedded in their psyche, first define their unique profile then look for people to practice it on. But I have found that approach to be an inversion of how calling is most frequently discovered.

If we start by looking at who God has already put in our life, then ask Him how we can best give them grace, we find the calling quickly becomes clearer.

My clearest experience of this occurred on a visit to the slums of Nairobi, Kenya.

It occurred at the end of my first visit to the East African nation. Some quite dangerous experiences in the country's far north had left me shaken. I was tired and somewhat jaded with the culture and all I wanted to do was get on the plane home. I had received no impression of long-term calling to this place, or sensed any sort of emotional attachment that might have signaled permission for an ongoing work there.

However, on the final day, during our last meeting in the slum district, I became fascinated at the difference between what my eyes were seeing and my ears were hearing.

I was looking out of the meeting place window into a literal valley of waste and sewage. It was a brutally hot day, but young children were relentlessly scouring the ground for any food scraps that might ease their hunger. I wondered at that moment if hell itself could be much worse. There was sickness, poverty, oppression and violence all within view, and no apparent hope of fixing it.

However, my ears were experiencing something altogether different. The locals with me were worshipping God enthusiastically in their native Swahili, being led in a sweet four-part harmony by leaders without any instruments. Their spiritual abundance seemed to overrule their physical hardship.

"Unikumbuke Bwana" was all they sang, over and over.

Suddenly, I heard the voice of God. It was so clear that for a moment it blocked out the sound of the singing.

He said, "I remember these people, I want you to remember them".

At that very moment, the singers switched from Swahili to English. They began to repeat the same phrase again English, and now I could understand it.

"Remember me, Lord. Remember me, Lord." All I could do was stand there, stunned.

It was too clear an order for me to deny. I had been given an assignment to serve these people despite my own sense of hopelessness and discomfort. I didn't know how, or for how long. All I knew was that these people were now my people.

Over one million souls were crammed in that one slum alone. I only knew two reasonably well—the married couple who were my gracious hosts. I knew their name, had become attached to their family, and saw that they were trusted leaders in the community. And so, it was them that I began to serve.

God showed me the people before He showed me my purpose.

On my return, a friend and I started a charity, and over the years God made it possible to raise over a million dollars for the work of that couple and two other couples God had made clear were to join us. That was it: God had six people for us to partner with out of the one billion who are suffering in Africa.

Of course, God's floodgates of provision soon became obviously miraculous. The continuing fruit is astounding, with so many lives being transformed. And that was all accomplished in our spare time!

That pattern of people first, strategy second, has been repeated throughout both my volunteer and professional ministries. Seldom has God defined in advance the specific project or outcome I should undertake. But He does give me, and you, people. They have a name, and a face and a future that sovereignly intersects with yours.

You have those people all around you already.

They are in your family, your workplace, your church and your sporting team. God has given them to you, and they form the greatest potential for kingdom fruitfulness possible. Your purpose is before you in the people you influence daily.

Whilst we might be tempted to focus our lives on a grand plan or worthy cause, we should be wary of any endeavour that lacks specific names and faces. An absence of human contact so often equates to an absence of God's presence and help.

On the hill in Galilee, Jesus could so easily have told the villagers to go their own way. He needed rest, the disciples were lacking training and there was a bigger picture to consider. And yet His compassion drove Him on.

People get *passionate* about all sorts of things, and Christians are no different. And yet Jesus was *compassionate*—having passion birthed from a love for people.

True love for God will ultimately have in its wake a love for people. Scripture, too, consistently connects our specific design and calling with those we bump into.

We don't need to look too far to discover our purpose. It is as close as your next conversation.

Pray:

Lord, are there people in my life today who you have called me to bless, and yet I have been looking right past them?

Help me to see with your eyes, and touch with your hands those within reach.

Amen.

Your response:

Has God ever shown you someone He wants you to invest in? How did He do that, and what was the result?

_____

_____

_____

_____

_____

_____

_____

_____

_____

_____

4.2

Your area of influence

> God has assigned you a boundary in
> which you have authority to impact.

READ FIRST: 2 CORINTHIANS 10:13–15

It is God Himself who determines many of the boundaries of our life.

We each have limits. They might be physical, emotional or relational, and so on. We can take the initiative to grow these various capacities over time. But some limits are set in place sovereignly by God's design and only He can alter them.

An example of this is the potency of the faith and the grace gifts that God has given each of us. Consider these verses:

> "Think [of yourselves] with sober judgment, each **according to the measure of faith that God has assigned.**
> … Having gifts that differ according to the **grace given to us**, let us use them: if prophecy, in proportion to our faith". (Romans 12:3–6, emphasis mine)

Paul clearly states that God has measured out the particular faith we have. He has also given grace—His empowering presence—in the form of unique gifts to serve the body of Christ. He also says:

> "But grace was given to each one of us **according to the measure of Christ's gift**". (Ephesians 4:7, emphasis mine)

The amount of empowering grace we have at any moment of our lives is in accordance with God's provision. We can't make more, and we can't earn more. It is totally up to His determination. You will have noticed that some people are simply more gifted and anointed than others. That is God's grace at work and we should celebrate it rather than compare or covet.

In today's reading from 1 Corinthians 10:13–15, Paul uses a term to describe another limit that we should understand—our area of influence. He says:

> "(We) will boast only with regard to the **area of influence God assigned to us**, to reach even to you". (2 Corinthians 10:13)

He uses the same Greek word here as he does in the other verses quoted above. That word is *metron*. It is where we get our word *metre* from, and can be translated as measure, portion, or area of influence, as it is here. Essentially it relates to having a defined scope.

Paul is showing us that God has set in place a boundary for your influence. It is the radius of impact you have in the world, as it relates to people. Your presence in the world makes a difference, and God has ordained that you have contact with very particular people.

No one else can bring the influence you can bring. You have unique thoughts, values and capacities that are needed if God's plans are to be fulfilled in the lives of those within your *metron*.

What is more, God has given you spiritual authority within your area of influence. You are His representative, assigned to re-present Christ by your life and grace. You are also God's holy priest, in the kingdom sense of the word (1 Peter 2:9). That means that God has placed you there as His ambassador, to invite the King's influence through prayer.

Think of your workplace, or school, or group of friends. You are not there by accident. You have authority to invite God's blessing and salvation into the area of influence He has given you. It doesn't matter if you are shy, disliked or unqualified—you have authority from God to make a massive impact!

So often we believers view ourselves defensively in our non-Christian settings. At work, we hope to not offend or stick out too much. We try to read the room and adjust ourselves to fit in so unbelievers won't think us weird. In doing so, we become expert thermometers, able to read the temperature and doing our best to stay cool.

But God has made you a thermostat, not a thermometer!

You are to set the temperature, not respond to it. And you do not have to do that by becoming that weird Christian with a Bible on their desk and an "amen" at the lunch table. You do it by stewarding the grace God has given you for that setting.

God is with you in that area of influence; you are not alone.

When you find yourself embedded in a secular environment, God is invading that space through you. You didn't leave Him at church last Sunday, or at home with your morning devotion. He is with you now—everywhere and everywhen.

God is in you, and He wants out.

You are His Plan A for transforming every setting in which you arrive. When you get there, the heat should be going up. He isn't intimidated by the swearing and negativity of the culture; He has put you there to bring powerful grace. Just as He does with your life, He is looking to redeem that setting and draw out the gold in everyone within it. He loves them and has a plan for them. You are part of that plan.

Many of those who understand this principle have seen the lives and cultures they dwell in change remarkably. I have known people who ensure they arrive early to their workplace and, whilst the desks are still empty, walk around the office praying for each one and blessing the environment.

Within days there is a noticeable change. Complaining goes down, optimism goes up. Spiritual conversations happen where they have never done so before. Even productivity has been seen to increase.

Someone close to me who is a school teacher told me how she saw this effect remarkably. She was posted to a school in a very socially challenged area, and the staff culture was known to be somewhat toxic. Her spiritual gift is hospitality and it became a powerful form of grace in that setting. She began praying through her classroom and the staff lunchroom. She brought cupcakes and gifts in as anonymous surprises for the other teachers.

Soon the headmaster called her in to the office and said, "I don't know what it is about you. On the days you are here, people who don't even know you make comments about how the whole campus feels lighter. The conflicts reduce and the smiles increase. Whatever it is you do, keep doing it!"

You are the spiritual thermostat in the area of influence God has given you. Whenever you are present, be it at home, church or out in the community, you can influence that setting for good.

And that influence can grow. Even though it is a God-determined boundary, He is willing to expand it for those who want to impact more people.

In today's reading, Paul was hoping to increase his influence with that church and region at Corinth. He said:

> *"Our hope is that as your faith increases, our area of influence among you may be greatly enlarged, so that we may preach the gospel in lands beyond you, without boasting of work already done in another's area of influence".* (2 Corinthians 10:15–16)

Within his area of influence, which was already large, this was a circle of people with whom Paul had specific impact. In acknowledging that God had given that to Him, part of his faithful stewardship was to ask for increase.

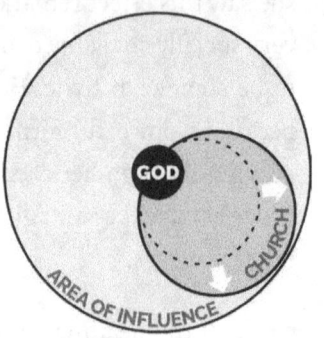

You can do that too for your own situation. If you have God at the centre of your life, and you are being faithful within the various circles within your *metron*, God will often grant more influence.

An Old Testament man called Jabez prayed this way too, and God blessed it. He said:

> *"'Oh that you would bless me and enlarge my border, and that your hand might be with me, and that you would keep me from harm so that it might not bring me pain!' And God granted what he asked".* (1 Chronicles 4:10)

People are your purpose. God has placed many within your effective radius and they make up the foundation and focus of your calling in Christ. Before we seek new or greener fields, we should ensure we are watering the field we are already in.

Is God calling you to take up the mantle He has already placed on you to impact those already at hand?

Pray:

Lord, thank you that the fields in which I dwell are already ripe for harvest.

I am your worker right there. Help me to faithfully steward the grace you have given me for each setting.

Amen.

Your response:

Is there a group of people God has placed you in that you could increasingly influence for God? How might you best do that?

_____

_____

_____

_____

_____

_____

_____

_____

4.3

You and the church

To find the fullness of God's calling on your life,
you also need to find yourself in church.

READ FIRST: 1 CORINTHIANS 12

Within the broader area of influence given to you by God is another circle of impact—the Christian church.

If Christ lives in you, then you are a part of the church globally—and there are no spare parts in His body. He has sovereignly equipped you to play a part in the church, and that function is an intrinsic part of your life's calling. If, for whatever reason, you are disconnected from the church, then you are missing out, and so are they.

The church is this age's fulfillment of the grandest endeavour the world has seen.

It began with Abraham, about 2000BC, when God called a man out of his idolatrous culture to birth a nation of faith. God's plan was to call as His own a people who would be a sign to the world of the goodness of God. They were to exemplify the kingdom, a culture where God reigned. Later, at Mt Sinai, these people were called to be a kingdom of priests and a holy nation (Exodus 19:6).

God's people were always meant to stick out—that was the point. They were to exemplify what could and should be. And they were to be identified, as Abraham was, as those who relied on God to redeem and resource.

The term "kingdom of priests" faded at the Exodus, however. The Hebrews were prepared to be God's people, but they held up a hand to the idea of God's imminence. They were drawn to idols and preferred that God stayed at a discreet distance (Exodus 20:18–19).

That was the day the law was given, and it was celebrated annually at what became known as the Feast of Pentecost. Even though it was a moment where they rejected the offer to be a kingdom of priests, they held strongly to the commandments and the leadership of Moses.

The trouble was, and remains, that you can't fulfil your call to be God's people if you keep God at a distance. A people of faith is by design a people of proximity. For you to rely on God, you must be connected to Him. You can't draw from His supply if you are not abiding in the Vine.

Therefore, after Christ had risen, it was this same Feast of Pentecost that He determined was the moment to birth the church. Where they had once insisted that God stay apart, He now brought His Spirit to be within each. From that moment, God's church was also given the name offered in Exodus 19:6:

*"But you are a chosen race, a **royal priesthood**, a holy nation, a people for his own possession, that you may proclaim the excellencies of him who called you out of darkness into his marvelous light".* (1 Peter 2:9, my emphasis)

God's dream of establishing a people who might proclaim His excellencies through word, deed and culture was back in play. And you are part of that dream.

Significantly, at Pentecost a flame resided on the head of every believer, symbolising the presence of the Spirit within each one. There were to be no spectators in this kingdom; everyone was anointed to be involved.

There is nothing like the local church when it gets it right. Lost people get found, found people grow, hearts are healed, and passionate purpose is realised in those who invest deeply.

There is also nothing quite as disappointing as experiencing church when it goes wrong. People are hurt, communities remain un-pastored, and the name of Christ is smothered by the cobwebs over the front door.

It's never difficult to find a reason, or blame a particular person, for our disappointing experiences with God's people. Hang around anyone for long enough and you will experience their imperfection. We must work incredibly hard, however, at not abdicating our own purpose in God because of the actions and perceived intent of others.

We cannot forget the fundamental element that defines God's people—the fact that together they rely on God. We are to stay connected to people, but not place faith in them as we do our heavenly Father. They let us down, He never will.

In the places where churches are thriving, it is because the people within them are deeply committed to playing their part. They have put aside their consumerist approach, and plunged-in sacrificially. When the inevitable disappointments and imperfections arise, their buy in and commitment overrules their desire to disconnect.

You need to be engaged in the life of your church.

Whether it be in an official role or as a free agent investing into the lives of others, God has given you gifts, abilities and experiences that build up God's people.

> *"To each is given the manifestation of the Spirit for the common good."* (1 Corinthians 12:7)

It can be challenging to find your place at times, indeed it is usually something of a journey. The role may change with the seasons of life, correlating with your family dynamics or growth in new skills. Often, we have no idea of what our sweet-spot might be, and so we need to experiment, or simply turn up prepared to sacrificially give.

It is the determination to serve wherever we are needed which so often triggers a more obvious sense of guidance. We find our calling when we find our people.

My own journey into vocational ministry started this way. Having run my own business for some time, I had determined there was little I had to offer the local church. And yet I was drawn by the passionate heart for God that some of our young adults were displaying, and found my desire to engage was growing for the first time in a decade.

They approached me to lead a small group through which to mentor their leadership. At first I refused, believing I lacked the skills they needed. But they persisted, and I relented. Soon the group was flourishing and growing, with more people turning up than our house could accommodate. I never did feel equipped for that role, but because I had found my people, it didn't matter.

It was then that God began to speak and work clearly on the next steps of calling.

I felt a strong prompting from God while in a church service to wind up my present area of volunteering because it was now hindering what He wanted me to do. I had no inkling as to what that might be, but in short order handed over my role to one who had been developing well. Then, one afternoon as my wife and I sat in my office, we concluded that we should sell the business and serve the Lord full-time!

We hadn't told anyone this, but within days my senior pastor approached me with a job as a paid minister. That was the beginning of an amazing journey in Christian service which continues to this day. I have found gifts that I would never have dreamed existed, and seen fruit that boggles the imagination.

And it all began with identifying my people, and then doing what needed to be done to serve them.

There is just something intangibly significant about playing your part in the body of Christ. When we are rooted deeply in a fellowship of believers, building them up in love, it so often opens the door to the broader plan God has for us. If we remain aloof, disconnected, or invested into every other area of life, then we are at best truncated in fulfilling His plan for us.

Many people have a calling that is fulfilled outside of the church. We cannot deny this, and God has a plan for His people to impact every sphere of society. But, even then, I believe He has equipped us to contribute locally to some extent and, until we do, we are missing His best for us. Even those whose lives are dedicated to the cause of the kingdom globally through para-church, non-profit or justice-based organisations should set aside some of their potential to engage with people who they love.

You will not find the fullness of God's calling on your life until you find yourself in a local church.

Seek to do what you feel equipped by God to do. But if that door does not open, then serve anyway in whatever your hand finds to do. In doing so, you are trusting God that He can open doors that no-one else can.

It is Him you serve through the local expression of His body. Give God your best by giving His body your best.

Pray:

Lord, thank you that I get to serve you by serving your people.

Show me where I am best utilised, and may your grace and gifts be useful in building up your church.

Amen.

Your response:

Where are you serving in the local church? Is there another way you would like to contribute? What steps could you take to fulfil that?

_____

_____

_____

_____

_____

4.4

Oikos

Your greatest calling is to those who are closest to you.

READ FIRST: ACTS 16:25–34

How could Paul say with such confidence to the Philippian jailer, "Believe in the Lord Jesus, and you will be saved—you and your household"? (Acts 16:31).

Did salvation suddenly become reliant on who you were related to? Did one person in the family making a choice for Christ give the others a free pass by proxy?

Or did Paul have a word of prophetic insight? Might God have whispered to him that the outcome would be a household revival? The text doesn't infer that, and it would be questionable exegesis to suggest as much.

How then could Paul be so certain?

Perhaps he knew by observation what we now know by statistical evidence—that 95% of those who come to Christ do so through their close connection with someone who has already made that choice.

It is those who know us very well, and who see demonstrable transformation in us, who are most frequently moved to believe. You just cannot deny the evidence of a life changed, and it is those close to us who see the effects of salvation most clearly. You can't fool them; they know your limitations, strengths and foibles. And when God does a work in us that shifts our heart, it shifts theirs too.

As former President Ronald Reagan said in his farewell address to the nation, "All great change in America begins at the dinner table". It is those we do life with daily who hold the greatest potential for our influence.

It isn't great speeches or sermons. It's not convincing rhetoric or the threat of judgment that inspires change—it is the demonstrable proof that change is both possible and preferable in those closest to us.

Paul simply knew that if a hard-nosed punisher like a jailer was prepared to submit to Christ, then anyone within his blast radius would probably soon follow.

The word Paul used for family in the original language was *oikos*. It is often translated as *household*. *Oikos* is a powerful idea in scripture and it stretches beyond the idea of blood relations. A household in biblical times consisted of immediate family (up to four generations), slaves and other people who did life intimately with someone. In other words, the people who see the very real version of you!

In our day and culture, *oikos* still refers to those who know us deeply and truly. But, for many, that is not actually our family, due to distance, dysfunction or death. Nor is it likely to be our list of social media friends. It may not even include the people you go to church with. It is the small number, maybe 8–15 people, who see you as you truly are day in and day out.

Life in the 21st century has put forward a new word for this *oikos* group: it is *framily*. Can you believe that is now a word?

Framily (a joining of the words *friends* and *family*) is used to describe those intimates who we choose for ourselves. It could literally be anyone, but they qualify as framily by their proximity, depth of knowledge of us, acceptance and commitment to who we are.

One would hope it includes our immediate family, as so much of God's plan is unfolded through the influence of parents and spouses. But many of us have fractured families or live far apart, therefore intimacy can be limited to those who live close by over time.

Our *oikos* holds the key to so much of our calling in Christ. If there was any environment in which we are a thermostat, it is our *oikos*. If ever there was a clear focus for the calling on our life, it is to impact our *oikos*.

Consider this. In the West, there continues to be a consistently slight decline in those who profess Christianity. There are exceptions, but at best the increase is less than one per cent for those places where a powerful witness is making an impact. This is despite the enormous increase of investment in resourcing leaders in how to grow their churches.

And yet in China, where Western Christian influence and resources were banned nearly 70 years ago, Christianity grows at an incredible rate. At the time our missionaries were cast out around 1950, there were 500,000 believers. That number now is 250 times that, at 130 million. At compound rates, growth still sits at 10% each year. Most of this comes through informal underground networks that exist without all the resources and training we rely on in the West.

How has it happened? The power of *oikos* is how.

Without access to media or large gatherings, all the believers could do was testify of their experiences to their friends and family. The example of God's undeniable work in each one became an incredibly effective testimony to God's reality.

It was the same in New Testament days before Christianity joined government and became a state religion around 380 AD. The world had been turned right side up by word of mouth, demonstrated transformation and the power of close relationships.

Your *oikos* holds the greatest potential for gospel impact.

And yet, what we see statistically in our churches is that the more time a person spends living within the Christian culture, the fewer people they lead to Christ! We might expect the opposite. After all, aren't we more qualified and equipped to lead people to Christ as we mature?

The reason for this unexpected dynamic is that, over time, the people we allow within our innermost circle are those who already share our love for Christ. We want the people who know us intimately to be those who have similar values.

In our early years as a Christian, things look a little different. Especially if we have come from an unbelieving background. Those close to us at that time are normally far from God, as we were. Therefore, a great impact is seen among friends and family as they marvel at such undeniable change. That is why so many new believers see those in their existing *oikos* come to Christ. As such, Paul expected that to happen within the family of the Philippian jailer.

The rate of change demonstrated by new converts is, at times, quite staggering. Mature believers, on the other hand, tend to level out in their graph of change over time. That need not, and indeed should not, be the case. There can be ongoing and significant revival in the hearts of believers throughout their whole lives. But Western Christianity has struggled to embrace the validity and power of the Spirit to catalyse ongoing and heartfelt transformation.

And yet, observable transformation of character is a huge factor in arresting the attention of those we know.

However, let's put that aside for a moment and assume that you have matured in Christ to the point where any further change is so incremental as to be unnoticeable by those around you. Is there another tool in your belt with which you can impact the unbelievers around you?

Yes, there is—trust.

Many people come to Christ when someone they trust invites them to embrace the reality of God. If the presence of radical change is absent, and yet trust is present, then credibility still exists quite powerfully.

This is where mature disciples really do come in to their own. If they have demonstrated integrity of character under pressure and over the long haul, then credibility exists. All it takes is a spark of interest, or a personal crisis of some sort, and those who know we are credible and caring will be drawn to our source of strength.

My wife and I once saw this at work powerfully. We had spent a decade or so investing into the lives of a group of non-Christian families we had met. For years they had tried to convince us that there was no God and that humans came from an ancient alien invasion of earth. But, we just loved them and determined to do life with them any way we could.

At one point, during a season "between churches", we became more available on Sundays. So we would invite them to the park to kick a ball and let the kids play together.

One afternoon, to the shock of us all, the most outspoken male amongst them put an old Bible he found in front of me and said, "Come on Pat, you are the religious one, see if you can teach us something from the Bible".

So, I did! I opened it up, read the first chapter I saw, and explained it as best I could in simple English.

The next week, they all asked to be taken to a church. We found one nearby and off we went. Amazingly, one husband and wife gave their hearts to Christ and were baptised on the spot. The rest made commitments within ten days.

That's the power of *oikos*! Ten years of establishing trust created an opportunity for ten days of revival.

The question is, who is in your *oikos*? They are your first flame front of calling. Fulfilling that might require you giving them years of unconditional love, or presenting a spiritual challenge, or having an openness on your part to your own struggles and faith.

Are there only believers in your inner circle? Maybe it's time to open your heart and home a little more so you can do life with those who need true life the most.

Your greatest calling is to those who are closest to you. Who is in that circle?

Pray:

Lord, who is it that is close to me that I should be praying for?

What challenge can I bring? What transformation in me would shift their heart?

Who have you put in my oikos for your purposes?

Amen.

Your response:

Who are the people in your *oikos*? It is probably between eight and fifteen who share space with you regularly, and who know the real you. List them out here.

_____

_____

_____

_____

_____

_____

_____

_____

4.5

Your tribe

We find unreasonable allegiance from
those who wear the same colours.

READ FIRST: 2 SAMUEL 23: 8–23

When Goliath was taunting the armies of Israel, there was not a warrior to be found. Not a man of fighting age would step forward in courage to take the giant on.

And then a teenage David came on the scene.

Within a decade or so of him beheading the giant from Gath, David had assembled a tribe of men so courageous and triumphant that the scriptures called them "mighty men".

Where were these men on the day Goliath was trash talking God and His people?

Many would have been present, but their courage was not. Not until they witnessed what was possible from someone with conviction, skills and a cause worth fighting for. They saw in David what could be, and what should be. They each decided that the place they needed to be was beside David. There they would have a reason worthy of them taking risks that might cost them their lives.

It is one thing to live for a cause—it is another level again to be prepared to die for that cause. Eventually, these men were prepared to do that.

In David they found their captain, and in the mighty men they found their team, their tribe.

Tribalism is at the heart of the human social psyche. It is the inclination we have to identify ourselves with others on the basis of a shared idea, language or purpose.

Tribalism is what compels an otherwise temperate office worker to put on a jersey, paint his face and scream fanatically at a football match. It is what draws middle-aged musicians to wear black T-shirts and a pony tail. It incites others to wear a leather jacket and ride a Harley-Davidson motorcycle.

Tribalism finds a way to say, "These are my people. They get me, and I get them".

When it comes to fulfilling your God-given calling, consider the unique potential of your tribe.

God is able to do in you more than you can ever imagine, and there is something about a tribe that draws that potential out of us. Who would have thought it plausible that a man would chase a lion? Before he met David, Benaiah would never have done it. What possible gain could there be in doing so?

And yet, that is exactly what Benaiah ultimately did. He was out walking on a snowy day and spotted the lion. But rather than retrace his steps to safety, he chased it down until it fell into a pit. Now, anyone else might stone or spear the beast, but Benaiah jumped into the pit and dealt with it at close quarters. He was going to kill that thing or die trying.

Obviously fear was no longer a determinant in how Benaiah made decisions.

History would record this man as one of David's most trusted and able warriors. He only found the fulfilment of his destiny as he was inspired by his tribe. Without it, he was just another face in the fearful crowd listening to a tall Philistine.

Not all tribes we join are such a positive influence as David's. Many of us allow our obsessions to drive us deep into a crowd that lacks a worthy purpose, or eats at our integrity. And yet, not every tribe needs to have an overtly Christian cause to be of worth. They can be a great way to engage with unbelievers and gain incredible influence.

When I took up cycling in my late forties as a way to gain fitness, I knew I would lose motivation if left to my own devices. So I invited a few friends to join me for Saturday morning rides. They invited others, and soon it was common for twenty or more of us to ride together.

A bit of healthy competition began to rise, and so we all trained a little harder to keep up the group pace. Suddenly it was costing me something to be in this group—I was actually required to exert myself! I knew I would soon need a better reason than weight loss if I was to go on experiencing such pain. So I challenged us all to create a charity ride to raise money for African communities I was involved with.

Soon came the "requirement" for colour-matched team jerseys. That was followed by a social media page and website. That progressed to event organisation and volunteer recruitment! Eventually, hundreds of people were swept up in this thing, and over the span of a few years many hundreds of thousands of dollars were raised.

So many people discovered a new-found sense of purpose and, dare I say, calling through the power of a tribe.

And there were other incredible dynamics formed that are unique to the setting of a tribe. The combination of unity within diversity was one. Those riders were from every level and segment of society. They were all shapes and sizes, had a wide range of professions, and many came from varied religious backgrounds. And yet, because of our joint interest and time spent, there was an unspoken expectation of acceptance and loyalty.

A mechanic from that tribe felt free to get advice from a lawyer. The lawyer got access to special medical services. The Christian pastor got to pray for the atheist. We freely exchanged with each other those things that were not available to those outside the tribe.

It sounds much like the early church in Acts 2. Even though they came from all walks of life, they shared everything, met regularly and protected each other at all costs. Like David's mighty men, they were prepared to stand back to back and defend someone they would otherwise have little contact with.

This almost unreasonable allegiance that forms in tribes provides a powerfully open door for the gospel. Because of the inherent sense that fellow tribe members accept us, we are far more willing to listen to what otherwise might remain unheard. Tribes give us the chance to fast-track the journey of gaining credibility and to share our world with those so different to us.

People who find their tribe are often able to achieve incredible things together. They have the benefit of singular purpose, which means they don't spend a lot of energy dealing with opposing views. They just get on with the cause that brought them together. Their cause. The cause they are interested in.

In some ways, our tribe, when we find one, can become a little threatening to our other friends and family. Inevitably we find that those in our tribe are not always those in our *oikos*. We must, therefore, carefully manage the role our tribes play in our own heart and life. Our investment in them must be intentionally determined and not be at the expense of those who truly know and love us.

Because they are joined around a cause, there is often little accountability of people's personal lives within tribes. Something of a "don't know and don't care" attitude can be adopted because they are joined around something separate from that. But sadly, many families have been lost over an excessive commitment to those who wear our tribal colours.

And yet, in its proper place, the tribe is a great mechanism for living out your purpose. Like most things, however, they may come and go within the seasons of life.

In my own case, whilst I still enjoy cycling, I have returned to riding with just a few friends. I have other assignments to fulfil now.

As a senior pastor, I have many circles of influence that need to be managed responsibly. Like you, I have my *oikos* of family and close friends. I also lead a church that requires more focus and prayer than most other careers. And yet, I know that I really find my sweet-spot when involved in a tribe. I need to be with my own people!

I had to find a way for that to fit in with my existing activities of ministry. The solution was to form my current tribe which I call the "Spirit and Truth community". It is a growing group of believers, many from my own church, who gather weekly at our campus to worship freely, give and receive ministry, and grow in our use of the gifts of the Holy Spirit.

It is that community that has inspired my writing and started lots of other projects that would not have otherwise seen the light of day.

But, what about you?

Do you have a tribe that you resonate easily with? Maybe you don't yet, but know it's time to invest in something new. Maybe you do have a tribe, but need to re-assess whether it is healthy for you stay there. Or, perhaps you are in just the right place already, and just need to invest intentionally in redeeming that situation for God's purposes.

God has woven the desire to belong into each of us. Find your tribe, and help others to belong as well.

Pray:

Lord, who do I naturally resonate with?

What is my tribe, and where can I find it?

Help me to be your person fully in that setting, and to fulfil your purposes.

Amen.

Your response:

Who is your tribe? What has it added to your life, and how have you added to those within it?

4.6
re:FOCUS on people

*God needs to be the centre of our life
and present in all our relationships.*

READ FIRST: MATTHEW 22:36–40

The primary focus of calling is to love God with all that we have—heart, soul, strength and mind.

How are you doing with that?

It is very tempting to want to tick that box too quickly and to move on to the next priority. The reality, however, is that you will never fulfil the rest of your calling if that foundation is insufficient.

Our love *for* God gives us the motivation to love people. It's the love *of* God within us that makes loving people possible. You cannot separate the two.

If you are running out of love for people, it often means your love for God is not transforming and fueling you as it can.

You certainly may love God, but for some reason that love isn't connecting with those people. What you need to do is connect the circles—to ensure God is the common denominator in every area of life.

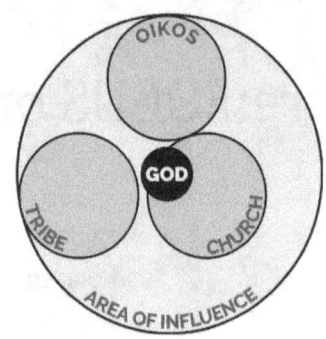

This week, we have discussed the various circles of relationships you have in your life. There is your overall area of influence, your church, your *oikos* and your tribe.

It is possible to get these areas somewhat out of focus. If God's influence is not with you in any one of those circles, then in that area you will bear no kingdom fruit. Jesus was clear that without abiding in Him we can do nothing (John 15:5).

If, for example, we have our tribe and yet we do not pray for them or allow God to be part of that circle, then it is largely wasted for His purpose. If that circle is also separated from the other areas of our life, it can be dangerously lacking in accountability and balance.

There should be no area of life where we do not invite the influence of God to make a difference. And where at all possible, we should have a degree of people-overlap, regardless of size, between each area. Our family should experience church life with us. Likewise, we benefit if our close friends are part of our tribe as well. We shouldn't partition ourselves off into separate lives.

We only have one life and one God. As such, He expects to be Lord of everything. We can't assume that because God is part of our church life and family that He has no say in our hobbies.

Life is so much simpler and fruitful when we refocus our contact with people. This is the ideal.

Sadly, for some this is simply not possible, at least in a relational sense. Our spouses may remain unsaved and our children unexposed to positive Christian peers. But we can still bring God's influence to bear by prayer. This can never be underestimated!

> *"For the unbelieving husband has been sanctified through his wife, and the unbelieving wife has been sanctified through her believing husband… How do you know, wife, whether you will save your husband? Or, how do you know, husband, whether you will save your wife? Nevertheless, each person* **should live as a believer in whatever situation the Lord has assigned to them**, *just as God has called them."* (1 Corinthians 7:14-17, emphasis mine)

Those we are connected with are sanctified, Paul says. This means they are set apart for God. They must still make their own decisions for God, but God has them singled off as prime targets!

I have found that for those I am in contact with who do not allow overt Christian conversation to take place, I can pray with authority because they are already in God's cross-hairs. I am the closest one to them that carries God's Spirit. They are within my legal area of influence!

I can pray scriptures over them, such as Ephesians 3:16–19, that God would reveal to them the incredible size of His love. More than one unbelieving soul has found Christ through this strategy.

Once we have the faith and focus to get our relational circles in place, we can begin to really get traction!

God wants us to become ever more fruitful. And that requires an increase of His influence. For any circle of influence to grow, the influence of God first needs to grow in us. That is the process we discussed last week, that of character growth. When a Christian grows in the depth of their character, what they are essentially increasing is the fruit of God's Spirit.

That is why character growth is part of your calling—it ensures your fruit increases.

If you want to see your family, friends and work associates come to Christ, then make sure you are praying for more of God to be exhibited in your own life. It's a vital part of the plan.

This dynamic alone, if given the fullness of our passion, would so multiply the influence of God in our world that it would be unrecognisable. If God's people would squeeze the most out of their existing potential to host God's presence in their own life and situation, it would be doubtful that they would be asking God about their next step of calling. AW Tozer once said:

> *The world is perishing for lack of the knowledge of God and the Church is famishing for want of His Presence.*[1]

One must wonder why we would ask God to lead us on to new, or more, or greater things when the influence of the Greatest One is not yet fully realised in our personal life. What we inevitably find, however, is that increase of impact does [or will] happen when we embed ourselves fully in what God is doing in our circle of influence.

It is just His way. If He is more present in us, then the blast radius of that will have to fan out. As Paul says in 2 Corinthians 10:15, "Our hope is that, as your faith continues to grow, our sphere of activity among you will greatly expand".

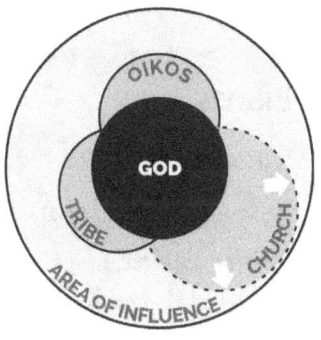

There is no shortage of things God would love to see accomplished on earth. His desire to impact the human race for His redemptive purposes far outstrips our ability to keep up.

He longs to continually increase the fruit in the lives of those who love Him. But His will can only be fulfilled in His way, which is that we adhere to the principle of "Christ in us, the hope of glory" (Colossians 1:27). We are to love God, and the love God gives us in return is to be focused on people.

This is the dynamic of Christian calling.

If we are stalled in that journey, then we can look at how this dynamic is currently working within us.

Your calling in life is to influence people for God's purposes: to love them, save them, care for them and grow them. You can go deeper in that by loving those you already have to a greater degree. Or you can go wider by increasing the number of those you love.

These are the fruit you are called to bear.

Pray:

Pray along with Jabez.

"Oh, that you would bless me and enlarge my territory! Let your hand be with me, and keep me from harm so that I will be free from pain.' And God granted his request." (1 Chronicles 4:10)

Amen.

References

1. AW Tozer, *The Pursuit of God: The Human Thirst for the Divine*, Moody Publishers, Chicago, 2015.

Your response:

Are any of your circles of influence out of focus? How might you address that?

Group Session 5

re:FOCUS ON PEOPLE:

This week of readings (4.1 through 4.6) encouraged us to let our commitment to those already within our circles of influence become deeper. When we find our people, we have found our purpose.

Q. What was your overall response to this week of readings?

_____

_____

Now, discuss together your responses from this week's teaching:

4.1 PEOPLE ARE YOUR PURPOSE

> *When you find your people, you have found your purpose.*

Q. Has God ever shown you someone He wants you to invest in? How did He do that, and what was the result?

4.2 Your area of influence

God has assigned you a boundary in which
you have authority to impact.

Q. Is there a group of people God has placed you in that you could increasingly influence for God? How might you best do that?

4.3 You and the church

To find the fullness of God's calling on your life,
you also need to find yourself in church.

Q. Where are you serving in the local church? Is there another way you would like to contribute? What steps could you take to fulfil that?

4.4 Oikos

Your greatest calling is to those who are closest to you.

Q. Who are the people in your oikos? It is probably between eight and fifteen who share space with you regularly, and who know the real you. List them out here.

4.5 Your tribe

> *We find unreasonable allegiance from*
> *those who wear the same colours.*

Q. Who is your tribe? What has it added to your life, and how have you added to those within it?

4.6 re:FOCUS on people

> *God needs to be the centre of our life and*
> *present in all our relationships.*

Q. Are any of your circles of influence out of focus? How might you address that?

Conclusion of the group meeting

In closing, pray for each other that God would reveal new ways in which each participant can contribute to the lives of those God has given.

Week 5

re:FOCUS on Talent

You are called to give God all that you have become: heart, soul and strength.

5.1

re:FOCUS on talent

We all have a portfolio of God-given resources to invest in the kingdom.

READ FIRST: MATTHEW 25:14–30

What are you good at? Is there an aptitude you possess that allows you to excel in areas that others find hard?

When a person begins to seek out the next steps of their calling in Christ, this is often where the mentors and manuals start. It makes sense, after all, that God wants us to make use of the assets He has provided.

You will notice, however, that we have discussed three other important factors prior to mentioning our latent talent: your intimacy with Christ, your commitment to develop character, and your desire to love those in your relational orbit. Together they must provide the fuel for our focused activity.

If they do not, our energies can easily be diverted into endeavours that motivate us purely because we can do them well. Many Christian lives are expended on careers and hobbies that serve very little worth for eternity and yet bring a good deal of personal satisfaction.

Your calling is higher than that. You have been set apart as God's child and heir to advance His kingdom through impacting people.

> "For we are God's handiwork, created in Christ Jesus to do good works, which God prepared in advance for us to do." (Ephesians 2:10)

When we are squared away on what motivates us and who it is we are ministering to, the question of activity can become somewhat inverted. We need wisdom on what to stop doing, as much as what to start doing.

It is easy to become quite exhausted as we put our hand to every plough and steward a heightened awareness of every need. But, we need to be ok to say no. We must also understand that every activity that we pick up that is outside our area of giftedness is robbing another person of the joy of fulfilling their calling.

We are part of a body, after all. We don't help it become healthy if a lung insists on doing the kidney's job. We need to just breathe and let God raise up a kidney in His own way.

Jesus' parable from this chapter's scripture is often called the Parable of the Talents. Some translations talk in terms of bags of gold, but the currency of the day was talents rather than dollars, yen or pounds sterling. For us, it is a very convenient allegory for the discussion at hand.

The parable's point is that Jesus expects us to put to work the talents He has given us. As believers, our judgment will be based on our faithfulness (2 Corinthians 5:10). We are already saved through faith, but the shape of our eternal reward will be determined by how we have invested what God has invested in us.

If we aren't careful, however, the talk of judgment and the requirement for faithfulness can turn our discovery of calling into an overly onerous thing. We can come under the weight of obligation, fearful that we will not hear Jesus say, "Well done. Good and faithful servant". And so, we find ourselves frantically serving from the wrong motive.

God's heart is not to find fault and judge you. It is to set you free and make you fruitful. He wants you to find clarity of calling and awareness of what you hold in your hand. Implicit in the Parable of the Talents is the fact that we are not called to account for what God has *not* given us.

If you do not have a specific gift or talent, then you cannot be held responsible for it. In fact, time invested in an area God has not equipped us for may in itself be regarded as unfaithfulness!

God is not obliged to bless or resource an activity He has not intended for us to undertake.

The source of burnout for many believers can be traced back to them pouring their energy in good faith into areas completely outside of their call or design. Care-givers are thrust into ministries of leadership. Evangelists are forced to manage budgets or offer counselling. Acutely task-oriented people are encouraged to show more hospitality.

Our misplaced sense of faithfulness can compel us to so "die to self" that we almost die in the process. If you find yourself routinely burning out from the fatigue of Christian service, chances are you are working outside of your God-given strengths.

When we work in our area of strength, we tend to get stronger.

When we work in our area of weakness, we get weaker. Even though we are serving God from love and commitment, even the best heart can become jaded and dry.

This principle can appear to contradict the mandate we have to address the issues of our character. Indeed, we have shown in previous chapters that we are required to address the weakness of our nature.

And so, disciples might feel obliged to choose between worldviews—feeling compelled to either invest in growing where they are weak or preferring to focus on where they are strong. Different personalities will usually defer to one or the other. But we need to separate these principles out and apply the right one to the areas of spiritual formation and fruitful function.

Regarding formation, we work on our weakness. Regarding function, we work to our strengths.

Formation is all about the Spirit's in-working on our character. Function is all about the Spirit's outworking through giftedness and talent. Formation cultivates the fruit of the Spirit. Function invokes the gifts of the Spirit.

God is fully committed to both fruit and gifts, and so must we be. By allowing ourselves to gravitate either right or left, to fruit or gifts, we are like a bird that has strength in only one wing—we fly around in endless circles.

When we look at the portfolio of talents the Lord has bestowed on each of us, we can quickly see it goes beyond the overt grace gifts depicted in the New Testament. He combines those with our unique personality and temperament, our history and heritage, and the various aptitudes we possess.

Even our family, education and experiences are gifts. They build into us a set of values, presumptions and skills which, when breathed on by God's Spirit, are redeemed for His purpose. Nor can we forget the tangible resources He bestows on us by way of finance, possessions and physical ability. All are given to be invested for God's purposes.

These gifts, when tempered and focused by character, become the tools used by God to fulfil His plan.

When Moses was called out by God at the burning bush, he had no more significant talent than when he had left Egypt decades earlier. For his first 40 years, he had been invested with education, identity and leadership skills given only to those in the upper echelon of Pharaoh's court. For his second 40 years, he had endured the university of the wilderness, as humility replaced pride and misplaced self-confidence was eroded away.

After 80 years, Moses was now a man who could be taught to place his confidence in God, and to use all his talents to fulfil God's will in God's way. It wasn't to be just God, nor was it to be just Moses. It was to be a partnership. To show Moses how this new deal was to work, He said to him, "What is that in your hand?" (Exodus 4:2).

In his hand was a wooden staff. It was a person's symbol of authority and what they had achieved—an icon of what Moses brought to the table. God told Moses to throw it down before Him. Moses was to take his talents and let God use them.

When God was to do a mighty work, Moses was to lift his staff. It was a symbol of partnership.

I wonder what is in your hand. How many talents has God invested in you over your lifetime?

He could work without them, but He chooses not to. Like the young boy who offered up his fish to Jesus, it is that offering that is multiplied.

You have been given a portfolio of talents by God Himself. You did not determine the size and shape of that list. But you can determine what you do with them. They can be used for yourself, for selfish gain. They can be hidden away for no one to see. Or they can be invested for the kingdom and reap a reward.

Your God-given mission in life is to wring the most out of what you have been given. It is time to refocus on your talent.

Pray:

Lord, today I throw my staff down before you.

Whatever I have by way of talents, I give to you.

Show me where I can invest them for your kingdom.

Amen.

Your response:

What skills and experience do you have that God could use for His purpose?

_____

_____

_____

_____

5.2

Put your soul into it

Being faithful in your calling is about investing who you are into the very few things in life that matter.

READ FIRST: DEUTERONOMY 6:1–5

"Give it everything you've got!"

That is what the engineer shouted at me through the open window of my car. Thankfully, the car was anchored to the ground by heavy chains at the time. They snapped taut when I opened the throttle of the eight-cylinder monster I had created. The crowd of people surrounding the testing dyno sprang back as it threatened to break loose. The rear wheels were on rollers as the machine tested the horsepower of my latest engineering creation.

The noise was shattering as the engine approached its maximum revolutions. The exhaust sounded like a jet, and we could feel the air being sucked into the engine, seeming to crave ever more. The tyres were turning at more than twice any legal speed limit, while the car remained squirming on the spot, threatening to break loose.

The engine I had built for this car had the potential to generate staggering power. A testing machine was the only safe way to harness and witness its power. For the rest of its life, however, the car would be driven at a fraction of its capacity. As a novice engineer, I had created something that could never be allowed to fulfil its design. There was not a public road in the country on which I could let it loose.

Thankfully, God is no novice engineer. He doesn't create something or someone with wasted potential.

When He created you, it was to be an exact fit for this world and this time. Nothing was to be left unused. You are made to make a difference, to spend some time at full speed, and to enjoy the thrill of doing so. When God commanded us to love Him with all our heart, soul and strength, He was in effect saying, "Give it everything you've got".

But what have you got? What is under the proverbial hood of who you are?

Many of us have potential that remains unseen and undeveloped. It lies dormant, like a seed that just needs to be watered and fed for it to spring to life. Deuteronomy 6:5 mentions heart, soul and strength as three areas of our personhood that can be dedicated to God's service.

Your heart often refers to your deepest passion and core values that fuel you—it is the essence or spirit of who you are.

Your soul, on the other hand, encompasses your mind, will and emotions. There is a degree of inconsistency that exists in demarcating the human heart and soul as they combine to make up the unseen part of who we are. But if we were to say that the soul encompasses the totality of our unseen world, and that the human spirit is the predominantly unconscious element within that, then we have a workable model.

Your strength, on the other hand, is referring to your visible energy or physical exertion. It is how you tangibly engage with this world, its needs and its demands.

In this chapter, we will begin by looking at engaging your soul in the calling God has for you. The various talents God has invested in you are the assets which you can intentionally utilise. Your soul's intention determines where and how you do that.

By being clear on how the soul's mind, will and emotions can work together to build a fruitful calling, we can avoid the situation where, like my over-powered car, we are raring to go but can't go for raring. What I had done there was create a huge load of energy without any sustainable or productive way to engage it.

This is what it can be like if we allow our passion alone to determine our calling.

This may sound a little counterintuitive. After all, isn't it our passion that compels us onward to achieve things against great odds? Well, yes and no.

Passion tends to be a good servant but a fickle master. Passions rise at times and dry up at others. Desire can be fueled by all sorts of things, worthy or unworthy. My emotive drive can't be left as the main indicator of my calling. It would be like saying that I was called to hit the public roads at 200kph because that's the engine I had in my car. The engine is the one element determining the road, and any road will do!

What I should have done is look first at the roads, laws and destinations I have available in my region, and then design my engine to make the most of that. It is about determining a worthy future and looking at how my mix of available talents can get me there.

If we were to look a little deeper at our passions, we would see that passion follows action. If we invest a little in some area of life and have a good or pleasurable experience of it, our desire for it grows a little more each time. This, in a negative sense, is how we end up with addictions or ambitions that get us in all sorts of trouble. That is if the direction we are pursuing is unworthy in some manner.

Often there is no long-term intention to our efforts at all. We just put our hand up to try something and, with a bit of success and subsequent motivation, we determine to pursue it further. This is how many career and ministry paths take shape, for better or worse.

The great thing about kingdom life is that our moral code and serving opportunities present us with a worthy list of options to experiment with, as well as a clear list of things to avoid. These are formed by the preferred future given to us by scripture. We get to focus on what we know are eternal purposes and worthy dreams.

By default, this should become our way of looking at the landscape of life, and for determining where and how to invest our energy. We are free to experiment, but all the options should take us in the same general direction—kingdom fruitfulness. Without knowing specifics of our life-calling, we can be sure that our preferred future should be within the bandwidth of what matters to God. We can then refine it further to make use of who God has made us to be.

To put my soul into it means I start with my mind. I am to think clearly before investing all my energies into something that lacks purpose. I should clarify to some extent what my preferred future really is. Do I want to succeed in business because I am good at it? Or do I have a heart for impacting people and giving away money that is served by a business career?

Having a worthy endgame helps me decide what I say yes to, and what I say no to. The Spirit, too, will often provide guidance at this point, confirming choices made through faith and faithfulness.

Once my mind is appropriately set, then I should activate my will to pursue my chosen endeavour. My will is essentially my determination and capacity to choose. It is given to us by God, and He will not overrule it. And yet, when we use our will to pursue His purposes in faith, He blesses that by empowering our choice. The Spirit becomes the wind at our back, helping us go in the direction that agrees with His priority.

Our will should follow a clear-thinking mind. Whether we feel up, or down, or drawn to other things, we can remember our preferred future and make choices that keep us on track. Ultimately, if our direction is good and we are having a good experience of our efforts, our desire and emotions add fuel to what we are about.

This, then, is the order of precedence when discerning where to put our soul into the life God has for us:

1. A mind that has its priorities in line with the kingdom of God.

2. A will that chooses to invest in what matters, using the talents at hand.

3. Emotions that naturally spring from seeing lives impacted and the kingdom advanced.

From time to time, as we re-assess life, we will realise that what we are pursuing has had its season. We may have learned that it is perhaps not the best fit for who we are in God, or changed circumstances require us to adjust some things. We may even be spiritually and emotionally fatigued from over-doing it, having disregarded a healthy balance of working and walking with God. Our preferred future may not have changed much, but we need to look at how to navigate our course based on the altered landscape.

God is with us in these often messy transitions, although it may not feel like it.

In these moments, more than any others, our emotions are a fickle guide to determining what is next for us. It is here that we need to spend time redefining our preferred future with a mind that is thinking clearly, positively and under the influence of God's word and Spirit.

Giving it everything you've got is not a matter of recklessly putting your foot to the floor and keeping it there. It is about investing who you are into the very few things in life that matter. It is just as much about not trying to be who you are not. And finally, about not wasting yourself on things that are of no purpose.

Pray:

Pray along with the Apostle Paul:

I pray that the eyes of (my) heart may be enlightened in order that (I) may know the hope to which God has called (me), the riches of his glorious inheritance in the saints, and his incomparably great power for us who believe.

Amen.

Your response:

Are you living out what matters to you and God? Considering where you are required to invest time into career, family and church, are you satisfied that you have the balance and priorities right for this season of life?

_____

_____

_____

_____

_____

_____

_____

_____

_____

_____

_____

_____

_____

5.3

The heart speaks

Your core values determine what
you will and won't stand for.

READ FIRST: 1 SAMUEL 30

It couldn't get any worse for David. In the fourteen or so years leading up to this point, the only thing he hadn't lost was his life, and now he probably wished he had.

As a teenager, he had been anointed as the next king of Israel. He had gone on to exemplify courage and strength by killing the giant, Goliath, and leading the armies to great victories. It had been looking good for him at that point, and the calling on his life seemed inevitable.

But, as is often the case, there is a significant gap between anointing and appointing.

In fact, his life had seemed to go in exactly the opposite direction to what God had promised. His insecure king was bent on killing him. He was rejected by his nation, and in recent days had even been rejected by the enemies he had tried to help. Now, in his weakest of moments, as he looked on the charred remains of his home, even the men he had taken in and trained were lining up to murder him.

There was nothing left of David except his heart. His strength was gone and he struggled to know what to do. There would be no faking it or putting on airs and graces—the irreducible core of who David was would be seen by all.

If there were two words to define the heart of David throughout his entire life they would be *worshipper* and *warrior*.

As a boy he had played his harp and sung, taking time out to kill the occasional lion and bear. Ultimately, the warrior in him was to form the mightiest army of his era, and the worshipper would eventually plan the most famous temple in the world. His heart never changed, it just grew up.

But here in 1 Samuel 30, on his darkest day, the raw heart of the worshipping warrior would be seen by all. Rather than focusing on personal safety, he sought the comfort and strength of God. And once His counsel was found, David would set out to fight at a pace that few could keep up with.

Proverbs 4:23 tells us to guard our heart above all things, because everything we do flows from it. In that sense, our heart is somewhat non-rational. By that I do not infer it is senseless, but rather that the compulsions from our heart are not premeditated or adjusted.

What our heart cries out is often raw, unfiltered and unchanging. It doesn't consider the cost or wait until it's convenient. When we are at our weakest, that which is in our heart becomes most evident.

This is where our heart differs from our passion. David had no passion left at this point. He was emotionally and physically spent. Where our passions may rise and fall, or even change their focus, our core values remain strong for life.

There are just a certain few things within each of us that provide the tall river banks for the flow of our life. They determine what we will tolerate or reject, what we value and what we discard.

David could have given up at this moment that had crushed his spirit, but the warrior within would rather die than not make every effort to fight back. He could have pursued his enemy out of habit, but the worshipper in him paused to seek the face and permission of God. Everything he did was flowing from his heart.

And this rule of life didn't change when the circumstances were looking up.

On the way back to Ziklag after taking back his possessions, the men with David were against giving some spoils to those who couldn't keep up. But again David stood his ground, no doubt at the risk of his life. He insisted that each man should share the plunder, regardless of their input. Then David went further still, making it an ordinance throughout the land for as long as he lived.

This issue mattered to David and he would never bend from it. As such, the national culture was altered because of the personal culture of one man.

The core values in your heart have the power to influence your surroundings. They will cause you to speak up when the crowd is going the other way. They will incite you to defend a certain person or people. They will stop you taking a job that threatens what is valuable to you. They will compel you to invest big chunks of time into something that matters only to you.

Few people will attempt to steamroll a person of unshakeable conviction. The cost is too high. And so those convictions stand like immovable bollards, requiring the world to give way. If our beliefs only have a voice as long as they are convenient, then opposition or weight of opinion will snuff them out.

The difference between convenience and conviction is as significant as that of a thermometer and a thermostat.

A thermometer is an instrument used for measuring the temperature of the room. It responds to the existing reality. A thermostat sets the temperature, rather than reacting to it. Thermostats sense when a change is needed and initiate corrective action. Your innermost convictions will serve as a thermostat for whatever culture you are in. They will influence people's assumptions for accepted morality, priority and activity.

Identifying the core values of your heart is much like discovering true north on your life's compass. You can take your bearings and reset your course towards the few things that really matter to you. You will see distraction and frivolity for what they are and learn to simplify your lifestyle. If your heart can drive your God-given talents and personality, then you will quickly become incredibly fruitful in your life.

What, then, is at the heart of you?

As a follower of Christ, our first response to that question should be connected to the value-set and desires of God's Spirit within. That is what the early chapters of this material have sought to refocus for you. Your relationship with God, your connection to people, and a dedication to character formation should all be primary motivators.

We can tell if this is so by what you will be prepared to fight for. When David had stood years before, listening to Goliath slander the name of God and His people, it was a reality he was not prepared to accept. Either the giant would die or David would, but one way or the other David would not hear those words any longer.

What are the issues and values you will not bend on, regardless of cost?

This question may take some time to answer. For many of us, our irreducible core is not often under threat. Spend some time at the end of this chapter thinking back to the potentially recurring moments where you were prepared to stick your neck out for something. Was it truly important, or was it just an issue of preference?

Think, too, about the people you defend. Do you speak up for the poor? Perhaps you are drawn to the needs of single mothers, or orphans, or the marginalised, or some other group close to your heart. Why is that? Did something happen to you as a young person that triggers such a response, or is it motivated solely by Christian virtue?

David defended those in his company who could not keep up. Unlike their captain, these men's spirits and bodies gave way. And yet David had unbending compassion for those who others wanted to discard, and who an ungodly leader would ignore. It was a value for David that he had gained from the heart of God Himself.

David's heart incited him to act in ways that many saw as illogical. There were only so many ways in which he was prepared to advance his own cause.

At one point David's enemy, King Saul, was defenseless and at David's mercy in the desert cave of En Gedi (1 Samuel 24). And yet, despite the direct promise of God that David would be king, and this being the perfect opportunity to make it happen, it would have broken David's personal code to bring personal harm to the present king. He would never do so, preferring to leave Saul to God's sovereign dealings.

Some of us would make a stand for many things, simply because we have assertive personalities. It can be a challenge to distil our motivations when our first response is to voice an opinion.

But as you consider the question of your own core values, make the list as short as you can, until it becomes an irreducible core—a set of words that represents the people, beliefs and values that you will not compromise.

What is it that your heart speaks?

Pray:

Lord, what matters to you?

Help me to focus on those things, letting the distractions of lesser causes slip away.

Show me your heart, so I might show it to the world.

Amen.

Your response:

What are the issues and values you will not bend on? Beside each one, try to explain why it matters to you so much.

_____

_____

_____

5.4

The need at hand

When looking for your calling, look first
to what the world actually needs.

READ FIRST: ACTS 11:25–30 AND 12:25–13:2

Before his salvation experience, Saul had been a hard-core theologian and Jewish leader. His eventual calling, however, was to be most fruitfully seen among the Gentiles—those with no regard for the Jewish nation or their religion.

After initial persecution for his faith, he had fled to his home town of Tarsus and lived for 10 years or more in relative obscurity. That was until Barnabas sought him out. By then he had morphed from Saul to Paul, his name meaning the little one. He had once been a big guy in town; now he was happy to be no one.

When Barnabas eventually took Paul to the church in Antioch, he slipped easily into his known ways of teaching

God's word. It bore fruit, but nothing like the harvest God had in mind. To enter this new season, Paul would have to refocus.

Paul was doing what most of us do. We default to continuing what we know works and what we can do well. In those moments when we look for the next steps of calling, we might assume it will entail new or bigger ways to do the same thing.

To refocus, however, we may need to first broaden the lens somewhat.

God's call on Paul required him to engage with a very different world. The general principle that "find-your-people-and-you-find-your-purpose" needed a reset. Those who he was to reach were not his people. He hadn't even met them yet! First, he had to find them, then narrow the focus once again.

The skills and success we develop in life often come from a staged process. First, we experiment with something in the context we are in, particularly where we see signs of potential. Secondly, we invest more deeply, developing that skill into something specific that brings success. We might be tempted from that point to define our calling as that specific thing, in Paul's case teaching from scripture.

If we step the process back, however, we can see that it was something deeper in that first stage that compelled Paul to become a knowledge-filled teacher. The teaching was the fruit of a deeper root, and that root was his heart and talent for enabling truth to be heard.

When Paul had his first divine encounter with Jesus on the road to Damascus, his whole world imploded. Not because he was thrown off his horse, but because he discovered that much of what he had believed was false. Paul's heart was built for truth, and his old version had proven false. This would have caused him enormous internal stress.

But as soon as Jesus put His own truth in Paul's heart, Paul went straight to telling the Jews about it, drawing from his knowledge of scripture.

God had made Paul an evangelist for truth. But once Barnabas tracked him down, it was to find a new outlet. He was to move from teaching Jews to preaching to Gentiles.

God's call to a new assignment may require you to step back and rely on who He originally made you to be as a person.

As part of this process, Barnabas took Paul out of his normal surroundings to gain a broader experience of God's work. He went initially to Antioch, then down to Jerusalem where he witnessed key events: first, the homecoming of Peter after an angel broke him out of prison; then the nation-shaking death of Herod. God was at work in ways that were wholly outside of Paul's experience to date.

The world was changing, and God wanted His people to engage with it in a whole new way.

The goal of your calling is not primarily to fulfil a personal desire for significance. We get that from our standing with

God, no matter what we are doing. Calling isn't much about you at all. It is about being a part of God's current mission in the world. Our sense of purpose comes from serving His higher calling.

The question, "What am I to do?" should always follow the greater questions, such as, "What is God doing in the world that I can be a part of?" or, "What does my part of the world actually need right now?"

God is always wanting to meet human need and there is never any shortage of it.

The apostle's previous work with the Jews had been steady, but God wanted to go further and faster. He needed to recruit people like Paul and Barnabas who were prepared to step out of the synagogues and into the Speaker's Corner of pagan cities.

These two then came back from Jerusalem to the church at Antioch, no doubt impacted by what they had seen and seeking God for their next steps:

> "While they were worshiping the Lord and fasting, the Holy Spirit said, 'Set apart for me Barnabas and Saul for the work to which I have called them'." (Acts 13:2)

God was calling them to a new assignment, one that would not violate who God had made them to be, but would nonetheless morph them to meet the evolving spiritual needs of the fallen world. It would challenge them to the core for many years and cause Paul, particularly, to reshape his message to suit ears that had little concept of God or sin.

What Paul found in the world outside of Jerusalem and Judaism was the same as what we find today. Human need never decreases, it just changes its skin and language.

Inside us all, the cries of the human spirit continue to call out, looking to resolve the chaos that reigns as a result of the fall.

Those cries are sometimes for the removal of shame and guilt. Others are with a need to resolve deeply embedded fear or a sense of futility. Still more are with a longing to understand eternity and absolutes. These are conditions born of the same problem: separation from God. And yet they manifest quite differently.

People also continue to crave personal connection. The social media tidal wave has only exacerbated the need for people to meet face to face and be known deeply. Add to that the undying need for a moral compass, the end of injustice, equality for all and the eradication of poverty, and you can see the world still has serious needs!

In the place where world need overlaps with your developing talents and heart-felt values, there you find the seeds of calling.

The clarion call of Deuteronomy 6:5 is for us to love God with all of our heart, soul and strength. When we engage with the needs of our tangible world, we get to legitimately exert the strength we have.

If any of these three areas is to be the starting point of our quest for discovering our calling in Christ, it should be that of world need. It is the needs of this world that God has ultimately called us to meet and for which His supernatural strength is so powerfully given.

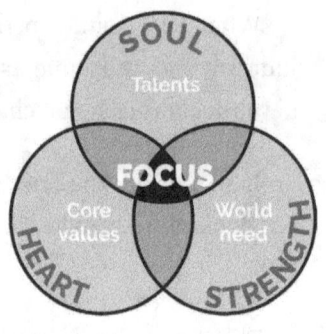

If we begin our quest by focusing on our own values or the talents we possess, we can quickly direct them to comfortable pursuits or those with an element of self-interest.

Under God's guidance, Paul set his eyes outward, beyond the church at Antioch and beyond the Jews. There were far more Gentile souls than there were Jews and no one had yet determined to reach them.

If Paul had not followed this path, it is doubtful you would know his name today. There might have been a by-line in the Book of Acts noting his salvation experience, but there would have been no epistles or tales of fruitful missionary exploits.

His incredible fruitfulness came from meeting the needs for salvation that surrounded him. Those same needs remain to this day, and God has placed you in this time and place to be part of the kingdom solution.

Perhaps, like Paul, it is time to avert your gaze from what brought fruit yesterday, to better see what is in store for tomorrow.

Pray:

Lord, what are the needs and people and places you have immersed me in? Where are you calling me to bring love and transformation in your name?

Amen.

Your response:

What needs do you see around you that you can contribute to?

   a. In your neighbourhood?
   b. At your work or school?
   c. With your family and friends

_____

_____

_____

_____

_____

_____

5.5

Spiritual gifts

> Your spiritual gifts bring God-sized
> fruit from your work with Him.

READ FIRST: ROMANS 12:3–7

God's will for your life is impossible to accomplish without His help.

This applies to your ability to live a godly lifestyle, as well as your ability to bear legitimate fruit for His kingdom. Any attempt to do either in your strength alone may well reflect human goodness, but not God-ness.

Romans 12:6 makes it clear that God has given each of us certain gifts. These enable us to fulfil our calling both within the local church and often in the broader context as well. Spiritual gifts, however, remain one of the least understood and applied elements of Christian life.

As such, the majority of believers resign themselves to doing their best with the strength they have. They try hard, do what they think is required and hope it is enough to make a difference. But look at what Paul said about his ministry methods in reaching the world for Christ:

> "I will not venture to speak of anything except what Christ has accomplished through me in leading the Gentiles to obey God **by what I have said and done—by the power of signs and wonders**, through the power of the Spirit of God. So from Jerusalem all the way around to Illyricum, I have **fully proclaimed** the gospel of Christ". (Romans 15:18-19, emphasis mine)

Paul didn't rely on words alone to convey the truth of the gospel. He demonstrated it through the power of the Holy Spirit. Only then would he describe his work as having been fully done.

There is certain God-ness required in our life if we are to represent Christ. Our testimony should not be constrained to what we have accomplished by our own potential.

Paul later said that the kingdom of God is not a matter of talk, but of power (1 Corinthians 4:20). Even though he was a man of words, he didn't want to rely on those words as his only argument. God is powerful, and He wants both you and the world around you to see the evidence of that.

Some of the main conduits of God's power working in you on a daily basis are the spiritual gifts.

As broad in application as the spectrum of human personality, spiritual gifts are unique forms of grace that enable us to do more than we could within our earthly capacity. Unlike other manifestations of God's power, such as changing weather patterns or raising the dead, the spiritual gifts are a unique partnership. We play a part and so does God.

If a person has, for example, the gift of generosity, then they must participate in handing over something. The spiritual gift shows itself by giving both the motivation and faith to extravagantly do so, and just as frequently provides abundant joy after the fact. The gift also produces supernatural fruit, more than our efforts alone could produce.

When spiritual gifts are properly used, both the gifted person and the receiver of the benefits will inevitably know that only God could have provided in such a way. They will, as 1 Corinthians 14:25 describes, say "God is really among you".

This sort of partnership takes practice to develop. Like everything else in the kingdom, the spiritual gifts start small and need to be developed over time. The most gifted healers I know all tell the same tale of small beginnings. They started praying for headaches and sore knees, often with no apparent success. But they were motivated to persevere and learn how to listen and cooperate with God.

Most of these same people have now witnessed the blind see, deaf hear and cancer victims go home cured. And yet none of them saw those healings when they started.

The idea of this process can incite offence in some people.

How can an unlimited God possibly be limited in how he works? Why would he choose to start small when He is obviously going to be glorified more by a larger miracle? It is this lack of understanding of kingdom principles that results in the huge majority of believers being unable to identify and work strongly in their area of giftedness. They think that in some way God just does His powerful thing without us being involved in any way.

It begs the question, how is that working out in the rest of your life?

When you believed in Christ, did you suddenly stop sinning? No, you had to learn the rhythm of repentance and belief, and over time the Spirit had more sway over your nature.

How about the fruit of the spirit? Did patience and goodness suddenly appear, or did you have to learn how to surrender to the influence of God in order to display the fruit of the spirit?

It is exactly the same with the gifts of the Spirit. Romans 12:6 calls them grace gifts, meaning they are activated by God's empowering presence from within us. And that is the problem, you! God's grace is working through you, and you are the one with limitations, not Him.

Think of it in the same way that a quality coffee runs through a filter into the cup. The coffee may be perfect in every way, but if the filter is full of muck, then the drinker gets less than perfect coffee and the taste of something else altogether.

You get to enjoy the lifelong journey of discovering and growing your spiritual gifts. All believers have them, and if you aren't actively utilising yours, then the body of Christ, and indeed the world, is not the place it could and should be. Without each part of the body playing its part, the body just can't fulfil its potential (1 Corinthians 12).

To identify your gifts can take some time. It is not like you get a spiritual position description and gift set emailed to you at conversion. Nor is grace stored up in advance for later use, able to be identified before it is needed. Grace is given when it is required for the task or need at hand.

You identify gifts most easily after they have been seen in action. You are to go about God's work faithfully, doing what your hand finds to do and meeting real world needs. As you do that faithfully, you will one day notice that the fruit of what you did was disproportional to the effort put in. Or, you find that you started a task and God finished it for you with way better results.

You come away thinking, "That wasn't me. Or if it was, it was not JUST me!"

If over time, and with the advice and confirmation of others, you determine that you do have a certain area of giftedness, then you can begin to focus more on that area of strength. God requires us to steward and grow what He has given, not wear ourselves out in areas where we are not gifted.

We grow our gifts by a combination of faithful practice, learning more about using them well, and developing more faith in God working through us.

Spiritual gifts are intrinsically connected to faith. If you knew your type and size of gift in advance, and exactly what God was going to do in any given situation, there would be little need for faith. But everything in the kingdom comes by faith. Paul goes on in Romans 12:6 to say, "If your gift is prophesying, then prophesy in accordance with your faith".

This principle applies to all gifts and not just prophecy. What it means is that you are relying on God Himself to work through you, without assuming in a carnal way that He is going to do just what you want or expect. You might take a step to bless someone, sometimes under God's guidance and sometimes purely out of faithfulness and love. As you do, you recognise the hand of God working with yours, or the mind of Christ leading you in how to speak or pray.

It becomes something of a dance, indeed a rhythm of grace. You work with Him, listening, following, cooperating.

In this rhythm, you play a part and so does God. You have seen this rhythm illustrated before, but nowhere else is it more evident than when working with God to fulfil His will in power.

You take a step, doing deeds faithfully, but knowing that unless God does something with you and through you it will bear no lasting fruit.

And so, you move from deeds to faith, making room for God to do what only He can do. When He does indeed begin to work, it's back over to you to steward that power graciously and humbly, inviting and releasing more.

The prophetically gifted person must communicate the message of God, and yet it is the person's own vocal chords and vocabulary we hear. It is the same with all the gifts of the Spirit—a divine partnership with frail human vessels like you and me.

My challenge to you as one who seeks to be living within the call of Christ on your life is this: identify your gifts and then invest in growing them constantly. This, by default, will ensure you are consistently able to bear fruit for the kingdom of God throughout your lifetime.

Pray:

Lord, thank you for the promised gifts of the Spirit!

Show me clearly what you have given me so that I might grow these gifts faithfully. Pour out you power in and through me Lord!

Amen.

YOUR RESPONSE:

Do you know what your spiritual gifts are? What are they, and how has God used you in that way?

_____

_____

_____

_____

_____

_____

_____

_____

_____

_____

_____

_____

_____

… 5.6

When doing it for God is not enough

Trying to fulfil God's will without sticking to God's plan can leave us high and dry.

READ FIRST: 1 SAMUEL 13:1–14

God's will is only possible when it is done God's way.

It doesn't matter how talented, anointed, called or determined you are. If you try to fulfil His unique purposes, then you will at some point need to rely heavily on Him to do what only He can do.

King Saul was about God's mission, fulfilling His sovereign plan. He was where he should be, when he should, doing exactly what the prophet had told him to do. And yet it was all falling apart.

The Israelites with Saul had developed a contagious case of cold feet. They weren't up for a fight they seemed sure to lose, and so they either fled or hid, leaving only a handful with the king.

He had waited for God, or at least His prophet, to show but there was no sign of them yet. Saul felt like he had stepped out for God and been left high and dry.

He didn't stop believing in God, but he had stopped relying on Him.

With that mindset, the best Saul could do was nod a polite head at God by doing the sacrifices himself. It was the exclusive role of a priest to do that and, besides, it was Samuel specifically he was supposed to wait for.

Can you relate to any of this?

You might have launched out on a cause with Christian intent. It may be a venture that the world needs and in which you are able to play a part. People tell you to go for it, and you believe God is with you. But somewhere along the line you seem to have outpaced God, going further and faster than He is.

Or perhaps you have taken a huge step of faith by committing to something you know is God's assignment for you. But it seems to have all turned south, with the only fruit being that people oppose you, desert you and criticise you.

"I am here God, doing what you said! Where are you at?"

This type of moment is potentially one of the most holy and profound experiences you can steward. Or, like Saul, it can become the moment you regret for the rest of your days.

You can look to heaven and choose to refrain from asking why. Right there, you can thank Him that He has seen fit to place in your hands a task that few could get through and that tests the limits of your faith. You can turn your critical levels of discomfort and disillusionment into the most fragrant praise, waiting for the king to arrive and do what He promised.

Or, you can revert to human logic and strength.

The vacuum left by the apparent absence of God's guidance and action can seem like an irresistible invitation to act. After all, perhaps you misheard. Or, maybe He wants you to keep pushing. Or, like Saul, you might conclude that God has no intention of helping you at all, but you feel compelled to carry on with the ceremonies so at least the venture looks godly?

The single most vital factor in determining whether this will be your finest hour, or your day of regret, is your ability to manage your heart.

What you are experiencing internally will be a driver for your actions. If, like Saul, you are caught in turmoil, fear and uncertainty, then you will do whatever it takes to escape that discomfort. God's response to Saul's actions was to seek out a man whose heart was turned toward God, not his own purposes.

Alternatively, if you are able to experience peace within the storm, then your goal becomes higher. You long only to seek God's face and stay within His favour.

One response leads to rebellion, the other to relationship.

Faithful deeds will always bring us to the point of exercising faith. That's the way the partnership works. And ultimately that faith will lead us to do something extraordinary.

Jonathan, Saul's faith-filled son, demonstrated this in the days following his father's failure. He set out in faith with his armour-bearer to take on the Philistines alone, sure God would act on their behalf. After they killed 20 men, the enemy took flight, and the whole Israelite army was inspired to overtake them and win a great victory (1 Samuel 14:1–15).

Just as our deeds are at times tested by God, so is our faith.

What makes it a test is that there is seldom a consistent way in which faith is to be played out. If there were, it would be no test! It is that very uncertainty of outcome that forces us to rely on Him relationally. We must listen, follow and wait on God, believing that He will do what He promises to do.

It took faith for Jonathan to go. It would take faith for Saul to stay. There is no formula, just a reliance on our personal relationship with God, being determined to listen and follow. And where guidance is absent, then we are to be and do what faithfulness requires—God's silence being as loud a message as His voice.

There are certain conditions of the heart which can reveal whether we are living in faith as we should, or in a state of unbelief.

Where there is faith, there is peace. That is not to say we aren't experiencing deep discomfort. But there is a foundational certainty that regardless of circumstance or outcome, God will give us all we need.

Where there is faith, there is joy. Knowing we are in close union with this God who loves us brings a brightness that the world cannot snuff out.

Where there is faith, there is union with Christ. The reliance is relational, inciting us to lean in and draw from God's love and strength.

Faithlessness brings out other fruit.

The inherent disconnection means it is difficult to stop and pray. There is too much to do, too many things to concern us. We feel anxiety and residual concern that things aren't fulfilled as they should be. Our life feels permanently incomplete and insufficient.

When our faith is disengaged, we are less willing to do anything or nothing for God. We present Him with our own options but don't seek Him for His. We become increasingly reliant on ourselves and, as a result, endure symptoms of emotional and physical burnout more regularly.

Ultimately, a life spent doing good things without God's help results in disillusionment with God.

Too frequently those who passionately seek social justice, an end to poverty and the eradication of disease are tempted to turn their back first on church life and, ultimately, on God. The apparent disparity between their commitment to a cause and God's commitment becomes irreconcilable for many.

And yet, God is all for those causes. Passionately so.

But we aren't called to do things for God unless we can learn to do them with God and from God.

Loving God and His kingdom with your heart, soul and strength is not a command to go it alone. It is a call to love God, not leave Him out of it while you get good things done.

There will be times in your life when doing it for God is not enough.

Pray:

Lord, did I leave you behind somewhere as I have set off to live for you?

As I look again at what I do for you, show me if I am doing it in my own strength.

Show me how to partner with you, and have faith.

Amen.

Your response:

How do you know when you are working from God's strength, and when you are not? Give examples.

_____

_____

_____

_____

_____

_____

_____

_____

_____

Group Session 6

RE:FOCUS ON TALENT:

This week of readings (5.1 through 5.6) brought focus on how to give our heart, soul and strength to God.

Q. What was your overall response to this week of readings?

_____

_____

Now, discuss together your responses from this week's teaching:

5.1 RE:FOCUS ON TALENT

We all have a portfolio of God-given resources to invest in the kingdom.

Q. What skills and experience do you have that God could use for His purpose?

5.2 Put your soul into it

*Being faithful in your calling is about investing who
you are into the very few things in life that matter.*

Q. Are you living out what matters to you and God? Considering where you are required to invest time into career, family and church, are you satisfied that you have the balance and priorities right for this season of life?

5.3 The heart speaks

*Your core values determine
what you will and won't stand for.*

What are the issues and values you will not bend on? Beside each one, try to explain why it matters to you so much.

5.4 The need at hand

*When looking for your calling, look first to
what the world actually needs.*

Q. What needs do you see around you that you can contribute to?
- d. In your neighbourhood?
- e. At your work or school?
- f. With your family and friends

5.5 Spiritual gifts

Your spiritual gifts bring God-sized
fruit from your work with him.

Q. Do you know what your spiritual gifts are? What are they, and how has God used you in that way?

5.6 When doing it for God is not enough

Trying to fulfil God's will without sticking to
God's plan can leave us high and dry.

Q. How do you know when you are working from God's strength, and when you are not? Give examples.

Conclusion of the group meeting

In closing, pray for each other that God would give increase to the God-given talents and the influence of His Spirit within each participant.

Week 6

re:FOCUS on Calling

Your plan must fit within God's eternal plan. You are called to focus on the purposes that matter now, and forever.

6.1

re:FOCUS on calling

Your purpose is found within God's greater purpose.

READ FIRST: ACTS 13:36

> *"Now when David had served God's purpose in his own generation, he fell asleep …"*

Our life only finds its meaning and fulfillment when it is part of God's greater purpose.

His purpose is constant and growing and our lives are to serve that great calling. Our existence is not a benign, encapsulated script that is isolated. Like David, our story is to be part of God's story—our meaning to be found within His.

When people lose sight of that, they quickly begin to drift. David's son Solomon experienced that. He began his reign with the wisdom to rule the nation. But once he was competent in that, that same wisdom left Solomon unhinged, leading him into ideas and practices that had no connection to God whatsoever.

If our vision for life is without a greater purpose, then there is little to stop that life drifting into meaninglessness, as Solomon's did.

If we do not grasp the greater reason for our existence, and the significance of the part we play in God's story, then any vision for life will do. We give ourselves to climbing a career ladder with no thought of the exchange value those years were worth to a kingdom cause. We spend hours in front of digital screens, being entertained by media, games or mini-series, unaware that human souls within reach are starving for contact.

A life spent without purpose must be the greatest tragedy of all.

However, when we commit to God's ways, we quickly see the magnificence and mystery of His eternal plan. This God who is beyond time has a purpose that is fully now, but also not yet. It is active and able to be tangibly embraced in the present, but it continues to unfold without limit, growing into eternity.

This is a vital thing for us to grasp, because so often we portray the purpose of God in such infinite and unattainable terms that we struggle to grasp it now or be motivated to even start.

For example, Jesus mandated that we go and make disciples of all the world. That mission is so big, and its end point so far-off, that we might lose sight of the present potential. In reality, disciples are made one person and one day at a time. You can fully participate in the mission this very hour and, in doing so, fully realise the call of God on your life.

The fullness of God's purpose actually has no end point. Just as he takes you eternally from glory to glory (2 Corinthians 3:18), so His plan will continue to escalate without end. A step of faithfulness now sets you up for an upgrade tomorrow. So, the sooner you start, the sooner you see increase.

Many believers lack this perspective, preferring to tap out and focus on things they can grasp now—the next step of a career, a better home or a new hobby.

As finite human beings living on the path of infinite purpose, it helps us to identify the next waypoint along the way. If we can focus on something that is this side of the horizon, it keeps us on track and inspired to take the next step.

We could call this waypoint a *vision*.

By definition, a vision is a description of what a preferred future looks like. It is a potential reality you could see happening if certain things are done. An effective vision is not set in the distant utopian future, beyond the horizon. It must be attainable, realistic, worthy and motivating.

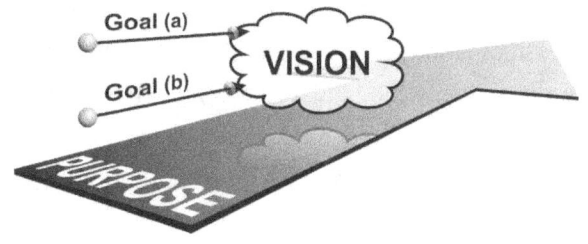

In the previous chapters of this book, we have unpacked some of the main elements of your calling as a human being.

You have looked at your relationship with God, the character He is forming in you, the people in your life, and the talents God has given you to steward.

Those elements only find meaning when they are connected to God's eternal purpose. They are the means; God's purpose is the end. In these last few chapters we will look at how to refocus those elements to form a personal vision. You will decide whether any of those elements require refocus and what goals you can realistically set to do that.

And even though your preferred future might be one or two years in the future, you need to reassess it every three months or so. You may even need to continually push out your dates or details. This is necessary for a few reasons.

Firstly, as you begin to progress and change, so will your perspective. As you refocus on people or prayer, for example, that which was important a month ago may no longer be valid. Therefore, you will need to adjust your goals to suit upgraded priorities.

Secondly, we need to accommodate the reality that life conspires against our best-laid plans. Something may happen that totally changes the landscape of your life, requiring you to scrap some things and pick up others. You may discover that what was thought to be a long-term calling was merely a seasonal assignment from God that has come to an end. Now He is calling you to another place and people altogether.

Thirdly, God will inevitably be upgrading His dealings with you along the way. The vision may be the same, but the methods need to be changed and the goals reconsidered. We see this clearly in the life of Moses. The God-given vision was for the Hebrews to enter the Promised Land, but that vision was pushed out some years as they proved to have insufficient faith or obedience to enter into that calling.

By believing the bad report of their spies, they delayed the occupation of Canaan and the immediate goal changed from migration to building a people of faith.

Moses, too, had to change the strategies constantly. What worked once would not work for him again. At one point he struck a rock to release water under God's guidance. Later, he wrongly assumed he should do that again. But God wanted Moses to speak to the rock. Failure to rethink the goal cost Moses dearly that day.

Finally, we need to reassess our vision continually because any human metric of what is possible instantly becomes a limiting definition of what God can do in our lives.

God is able to do exceeding more than we can ask or imagine (Ephesians 3:20). His purposes are ever scaling in grandeur and fulfillment. As we increasingly focus on serving His purpose, that which is possible increases as well.

This in no way nullifies the benefit of having a personal vision. Vision helps retain focus and gives fuel to the fires of passion in our life. But that vision needs to be surrendered to God regularly and not become a human-centric and self-determined end in itself.

Much of our ability to plan for the future is a process birthed in our ability to dream and conceive. God can certainly speak to us about the future, but He chooses in His wisdom to do that only on rare occasions. Much of tomorrow's landscape is reliant on our levels of faith and faithfulness today. God will not predict for you how little or much you will choose to either sin or surrender.

Ours is a life of faith from beginning to end (Romans 1:17). Detailed predications that overrule personal self-will would take away the need for reliance on God for every moment and circumstance. We would abdicate responsibility somewhat, saying, "It doesn't really matter what I do, God is going to have His way anyway".

On the occasions God does give definition to us of the future of our calling, it is usually because the journey from here to there will require the knowledge of that promise to get us through. Joseph struggled greatly between his dream of the family bowing to him and the reality years later. Abraham had to grow faith for over two decades to qualify for God's prophecy to come about.

Therefore, we should resolve to make plans that serve his purposes, and constantly lay them before Him for correction and adjustment.

Eternity does not begin when you pass away. It is now, and it is forever. It is time to refocus your life towards God's purpose.

Pray:

Lord, I rededicate my life to your purpose.

Yours is the kingdom, the power and the glory.

May my life bring glory to your name.

Amen.

Your response:

There are some other worthy areas of life that require us to set simple goals, such as fitness and health, recreation, finance and personal development. As part of your plan to refocus, detail any goals you want in place for those areas in the section of this book called *A Plan to re:FOCUS*, found at the back of the book.

You can download extra copies of *A Plan to re:FOCUS* from the website at *www.spiritandtruth.com.au*

6.2

What is the purpose of all this?

> God has given specific mandates with
> which to pursue His calling.

READ FIRST: GENESIS 1:27–2:25

God's purposes existed before time as we know it. The creation narrative in Genesis 1 and 2 shows the beginnings of our context within those purposes but, even before the earth was formed, God had a plan.

The fact that the angels existed, and that God was being worshipped by all until the pride-oriented fall of Lucifer, gives weight to the belief that one of the primary and eternal purposes of all creation is to glorify God.

Some scholars have defined the purposes of God in terms of the *Missio Dei*—the Mission of God. Traditionally, Christians have thought of mission in terms of bringing salvation to people or peoples, but the *Missio Dei* is a grander concept whereby God Himself is defined as missional. His people, the church, are seen as agents of His mission and are destined to extend it wherever possible. Alan Hirsch says, "To obstruct this (*Missio Dei*) is to block God's purposes in and through God's people"[1].

God's purposes existed before humanity's need for redemption. Our salvation opens the door to fulfil that which came before and will continue past this age of brokenness and pain. It has been said that "the end result of such *Missio Dei* is the glorification of the Father, Son and the Holy Spirit"[2].

We can see that the definition of God's kingdom is not limited to an experience of salvation: the provision of a proverbial ticket to heaven when we die. The kingdom is that realm where the king has domain (king-dom) and where His perfect will is done. As God's heirs, we are stewards and subjects of that kingdom.

The realisation of the kingdom of God is seen most clearly in the created order of the Garden of Eden in Genesis 1 and 2. There, God's purpose was seen without blemish. When we consider the front and back pages of scripture, we can see that it is effectively Eden that we will return to after the final judgment.

That created order can be defined in its most simple terms as *shalom*, often translated as *peace*. Shalom goes much deeper than signifying a lack of conflict. Cornelius Plantinga Jr describes shalom in this way:

> *The webbing together of God, humans, and all creation in justice, fulfillment, and delight is what the Hebrew prophets call shalom. We call it peace, but it means far more than mere peace of mind or a cease-fire between enemies.*
>
> *In the Bible, shalom means universal flourishing, wholeness and delight – a rich state of affairs in which natural needs are satisfied and natural gifts fruitfully employed, a state of affairs that inspires joyful wonder as its Creator and Savior opens doors and welcomes the creatures in whom he delights. Shalom, in other words, is the way things ought to be.*[3]

This is a description of how it looks when God's purposes are fulfilled. But can you see that shalom is not a static state? It is dynamic and growing. Eden was never meant to remain just as it was in Genesis 1. God's people were to both enjoy shalom and extend it into the largely blank canvas of creation.

The garden itself was relatively small, but we were to make the world look more like that. We were free to expand and create. We were to govern, cultivate and invent. Perhaps we could wrap up all these concepts and definitions in the following way:

> *God's purpose is fulfilled in us when He is glorified through an experience and extension of shalom.*

This definition takes us beyond this phase of creation's story. As long as we exist, both in this life and the next, this is what we are to be about.

This is truly a lofty, never-ending and ever-growing purpose. One which we need to break down a little if we are to have any hope of grasping and applying ourselves to it meaningfully. Thankfully, God Himself gives us some concise mandates which allow us to both refocus and assess our dedication to God's purpose.

The first is found originally in Deuteronomy 6:5 and was confirmed by Jesus in the New Testament context. It is:

> *"Love the LORD your God with all your heart and with all your soul and with all your strength".*

Before anything else, we are to literally give God everything we have and commit ourselves to His purpose. Love for Him is not to be fitted in to the rest of our life—He is to be our life. Jesus would often follow this command with the next mandate:

> *"Love your neighbour as yourself".* (Matthew 22:40)

Jesus went on to say that every law is summed up by these two commands. Love for people will always follow in the wake of genuine love for God. These two ancient mandates never change or fail but, in His context of ushering in a new covenant, Jesus added to the list:

> *"A new command I give you: Love one another. As I have loved you, so you must love one another".* (John 13:34)

Jesus is speaking to the disciples here and, in effect, to all believers. He is giving a specific command to believers that we give special focus to each other, loving and serving the church. He gave us gifts specifically to build each other up and to ensure that no Christian sees themselves as an island. Finally, Jesus also gave us the mandate to:

> *"Go and make disciples of all nations, baptising them in the name of the Father and of the Son and of the Holy Spirit".* (Matthew 28:19)

We are to be about God's redemptive mission of bringing people into relationship with Christ so they might become like Him. In this sense, evangelism is part of discipleship in that salvation is but one step of an eternal journey with God.

These four mandates are the primary imperatives by which we gauge success in fulfilling the purpose of God. They can be expanded and explained almost indefinitely, but by achieving them we are essentially being about the purpose of glorifying God through an experience and extension of the kingdom.

But note how enormous and unconstraining the mandates are. The fulfillment of them in our day looks radically different to the era in which they were first given. And yet we can personally fulfil them at any time, just as they did. Gods purpose is fully now, but not yet—able to be experienced in the present, and yet ever-growing and seemingly out of reach.

The way we actually achieve those mandates is worked out through our calling. We embrace our life in God's purpose by growing in union with Christ, developing Christ-like character, serving our people and using our God-given talents.

As you define your preferred future and subsequent goals for these areas over the next few chapters, we can use the mandates above as a final test. We can assess our goals to see whether they fulfil or counter the mandates and adjust them if necessary.

Our goals are what matter least. They must serve the greater purpose.

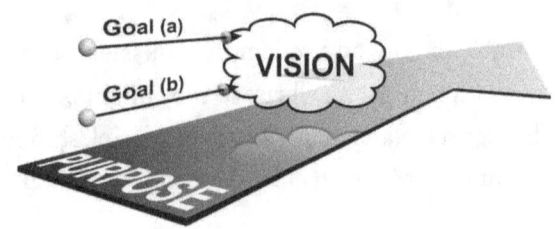

We only persevere in achieving goals if there is a motivating reason to pursue them. We need to know the "why" before we buy in to change or discomfort.

God's purpose provides that "why". The grand endeavor of joining Him in His eternal mission is enough to motivate the sleepiest heart.

Pray:

Lord, increase my vision! Lift my eyes to see and appreciate the magnitude of what you call me to.

I want to dedicate myself to glorifying you through an experience and extension of shalom.

Amen.

REFERENCES

1. A Hirsch, *The Forgotten Ways*, Brazos Press, Grand Rapids, MI, 2006, 82.

2. GW Peters, *A Biblical Theology of Missions*, Moody Press, Chicago, 1972, 9.

3. C Plantinga Jr, *Not the Way It's Supposed to Be: A Breviary of Sin*, Moody Press, Grand Rapids, 2009.

YOUR RESPONSE:

What does an experience of shalom mean to you? To what extent is it your genuine experience?

6.3

Whose I am

You are God's child and Christ's co-heir. Let that refocus your vision.

READ FIRST: ROMANS 8:14–17

Before the first human did a single thing, Adam was a fully loved and secure being. Everything He was created to do was an outflow of who he was.

He didn't become significant from what he did; his identity led him to do significant things. He was a son and an heir of God Himself, as you are. For you, that means the pursuits of the carnal nature and the ambition for worldly gain are not your concern. You have a higher calling. You are to find union with the eternally powerful and loving Father, and grow His kingdom from the power of that love.

When you consider your calling in life, it all hinges on this truth: who I am is completely derived from whose I am.

Early in this book we saw that the first element of our calling is to refocus on God.

You belong to God, and you belong with God. This is all part of God's eternal purpose. Our role is to live in accordance with that purpose, but that is where we easily lose focus. What are we to do about all this? How do we ensure we stay close when the world relentlessly draws us away? Your *Plan to re:FOCUS* found at the back of the book will help you do this.

As a starting point, I will distil each element of your calling that we have discussed in this book into two concise purpose statements. For each statement you can choose to form something of a vision for how it might look in your life, and then initiate some simple goals to help you stay on track.

Regarding our call to refocus on God, the first purpose statement is this:

I am called to live as a child of God—abiding closely with Christ, drawing my identity and significance from Him.

What does that statement mean to you? How could it affect you in real life? What are the implications on the state of your heart? What might it look like for you to grow so close with God that it changes your self-worth and security?

There are tangible aspects to this purpose statement that we can grab hold of and grow. For example, if I am to abide in Christ, as a small child does with a parent, then it requires time and proximity. I need to set aside quality time where I intentionally talk and attentively listen. I might need to be more comprehensive in the topics of conversation I have with God, inviting His input into previously off-limits areas. I will probably also need to develop my spiritual hearing, growing in my perceptiveness to hear the many facets to His voice.

Another aspect of this purpose that can be grown in our lives is the ability to embrace our identity and significance. This is often sourced from a sense of genuine security and safeness from God. Our inherent dysfunction and brokenness will distance us from this reality. Therefore, to abide more in Christ, I might need to bring my insecurities and fears to Him to be assessed and healed. Perhaps I need to shine a light on previously hidden addictions or judgments, asking Him to restore and rebuild my heart.

These, then, are the beginnings of a vision for a preferred future. You begin to see that there is a greater experience of this specific purpose to be enjoyed, and it will require intentionality to take hold of it.

And so, from there you can set some simple goals. You might want to deal with an issue such as shame or unforgiveness that you know is affecting your relational intimacy with Christ. Perhaps you will commit to working through a sister course like re:FORM to help you break free of issues in your life. Or, you may simply restructure your personal devotional times to include specific ways to engage God more effectively.

Take some time to think this through, then fill out the appropriate page of the *Plan to re:FOCUS* section at the back of this book.

Our second purpose statement to help us refocus on God is this:

> *I am called to live as a co-heir with Christ—bearing fruit through the power of His grace working through me.*

As an heir to the family business—that being the kingdom of God—your calling is to extend the influence of that kingdom. There are many ways to do that through word and deed, but one of the central ways we looked at is the ability for kingdom heirs to follow God's lead.

We are to say what He is saying and do what He is doing.

One of the least-developed skills of modern disciples is that of following the lead of Christ on a moment-by-moment basis. Developing the combination of perceiving God's still, small voice with the faith to act takes time and a lot of practice. Dare we mention, too, the inevitable mistakes that we make as we mistake our own intentions for God's!

We should not let this deter us, however. The path to powerful truth is sometimes discovered through bouncing off the walls of error. The lessons we learn from getting it wrong hold us in good stead as we press on.

When developing a preferred future for our calling as Christ's co-heir, we should take into consideration where we see Him leading us. Like a miner following a seam of gold, God might be taking us on a progressive journey to a more powerful and fruitful life in a specific area.

And so, your vision might take the form of you practising faith and deeds more often or more intentionally. You might set a goal for asking God daily to show you who He would like you to bless, and how you could do that. You might determine to pray for at least three people a week in their area of need. Or, you might set a goal for investing financially into a specific area of God's work.

As with the first purpose, spend some time thinking and praying about this. Perhaps you could talk it through with family and friends, getting fresh perspectives and ideas on where God is using you.

Then complete the section of your *Plan to re:FOCUS* called "re:FOCUS on God—knowing Whose I am".

Pray:

Lord, give me fresh understanding and application of who I am in you.

Thank you that I am a developing child and heir with you.

Show me my next steps.

Amen.

6.4

Who am I becoming?

You are called to be who Christ would be if Christ were you.

READ FIRST: 2 CORINTHIANS 3:17–18

The closer you dwell with God, the more like Him you become.

And yet, becoming like Christ is a completely contextual principle. You aren't Jesus, nor are you expected to live the life only He was called to.

You are uniquely you. God is continually forming you to be the specific person you are predestined to become within the context you find yourself in. When it comes to your plan to refocus on character, there are two purpose statements to consider. The first is this:

I am called to be Christ-like—the fruit of the Spirit growing tangibly in my life.

God is all about making you like His Son. This shouldn't surprise us since Genesis 1 declares openly that we are made in the image of God. As with most things God does, once His work begins it doesn't remain stagnant. He grows us from glory to ever-increasing glory.

When we come to Christ, the image of His Son is somewhat marred from the fall of Genesis 3. He has some work to do! And so, we embark on a lifelong journey of transformation, becoming the realisation of the name He has already given us, as depicted in Revelation 2:17.

The Christ-likeness we develop is more along the nature of Jesus than the unique personality He had. This is what the Fruit of the Spirit is all about, the facets of His character that we should all be growing in. Paul spelled some of them out in Galatians 5:22–23, saying, "The fruit of the Spirit is love, joy, peace, forbearance, kindness, goodness, faithfulness, gentleness and self-control".

When people look at us, these are the elements of Jesus they should see. If we are to develop a preferred future of the character God is forming in us, our first place to invest is in growing the Fruit of the Spirit.

What has God been growing in you lately? Have you chosen to cooperate with that process, or is it something you resist? If you were to cooperate more, how would you do that?

You goal then becomes simple—begin to practice living that fruit out in a specific area, in faith that God will, through His

Spirit, give you all you need to carry it out. This is the rhythm of faith and deeds in action—you take a step God calls you to take, knowing you can't complete it unless He helps you.

Dwell on this principle, then fill out the appropriate section of the *Plan to re:FOCUS* called "re:FOCUS on character—cultivating who I am becoming".

The second purpose statement that comes from a refocus on character is this:

> *I am called by name—being shaped by God into a unique person who is being, not just doing.*

When God shapes us, it often requires us to let go of something before we can pick up what He is giving. This is the shaping work of repentance, where we identify a behaviour or characteristic as something that brings death rather than life. In confession, we are agreeing with God that He has a better plan and an alternative way to live. In repentance, we turn from one belief or behaviour to something better.

This process is one of the few permissibly individualist aspects of Christian life. It is you He is building specifically. God's plan for you is unique and bespoke. Beyond the facets of Christ's nature that God is developing, there are those nuances of personality, appearance and talent that are yours alone. He is only building one version of you.

However, fulfillment of God's perfect plan for you is not inevitable. Only His dedication to it is.

Your cooperation is needed. You will, at some point, inevitably block His work through disobedience and brokenness. You will go slower than is possible, or you may even push harder than is sustainable.

When forming a preferred future for the development of your character, you can start by asking yourself, "What has God been trying to form in me for some time?"

Beware, you may not particularly like the answer!

That is because a change of that aspect of life will inevitably be connected to some form of discomfort or pain. God moves, and we often resist. This creates a sense of stretching and tension. And the greater the distance between where He wants us and where are, the greater that tension will be.

We try to avoid feelings like that. Pain always seeks pleasure, and so we might even find ourselves buried in prayers for comfort, when it is God Himself making us uncomfortable!

Therefore, when creating a vision for this area of character, an absence of discomfort cannot be a goal.

You could, however, determine to cooperate rather than resist. Rather than looking to escape a situation, you could commit to overcoming through it. Rather than fighting against someone, you could find ways to bless them. Rather than running from fear or shame, you could look for its source and bring it to the cross.

As with the other purpose statements, spend some time praying this through and asking God to direct your path in where to grow.

Then complete the section of your *Plan to re:FOCUS* called "re:FOCUS on God— knowing Whose I am".

Pray:

Lord, will you show me again where you are intending for me to grow?

Give me the strength to say yes to you.

Show me where I need to repent and believe in you.

Amen.

6.5

Who are mine?

Your greatest impact comes from loving and leading people.

READ FIRST: MATTHEW 16:16–18

When Jesus encouraged Simon by giving him the new name of Peter, there wasn't a single indicator to suggest that he would become "rock-like".

Jesus could see it, however, and made it his mission to declare and encourage out of Simon the potential He saw within. Some might call this discipleship—seeing who God is wanting to form someone into and helping the process along.

The task in Jesus' life that was second only to Him dying on the cross was to develop people.

Predominantly twelve people. That's all.

The disciples were His people, given to Him by God for a special purpose. There were others, of course, who were blessed by Jesus' proximity. His circle of influence would ultimately contain thousands, but they didn't have the same access as the twelve. And even within the small group of disciples, three were singled out who made up Jesus' inner circle.

Here we can see the three groups of people Jesus had in His life:

- **Metron:** the broad circle of influence Jesus had over thousands
- **Oikos:** the twelve God gave Him to grow. We might also include some of the close band of followers who supported Jesus such as His household
- **Tribe:** the three closest disciples: Peter, James, John. These three had exclusive access to experiences and intimate challenges (Matthew 17:1–7; Mark 14:32–33).

Our first purpose statement regarding our calling to refocus on people is:

I am called to love people—reflecting the heart of God to those around me.

When you have found your people, you have found your purpose. Rather than looking for greener pastures, we should commit ourselves to those people God has committed to us. I am certain there were people who were more qualified and mature around in Jesus' day that He could have invested in. But God gave Him those ones, full of dysfunction and mixed agendas that they were.

Some of the people God has given us in life are hard to love, impossible in fact. You aren't alone—even Jesus had a Judas.

We cannot fulfil this aspect of calling without God's help. We need His love to come through us. But that love must transform us, before it can effectively transform someone else. That is why we are told to love God before we love others. Jesus had to ensure Peter loved Him before confirming the call to feed His sheep (John 21).

When forming a preferred future for this area of your life, it should include within it a vision of you giving others the love you have first received.

If you sense no love for people, then part of your plan should be to ask God to help you see as He does, and then pray for those you struggle to love. Then, with sincerity and faith, begin to call out the destiny that God is committed to in each one. Whether they are yet believers or not, God has a plan for them that includes Him. You may be a vital part of that plan's next steps.

The second purpose statement to help us refocus on people is this:

> *I am called to lead people—impacting those in my circle of influence.*

In previous chapters (4.2–4.5) you have identified various groups of people within your greater circle of influence. They lie within your *Metron*, *Oikos*, Tribe, and Church.

Unlike Jesus' situation, the church is an extra circle of influence in our lives. As we saw in chapter 6.2, one of our mandates is to love one another in the household of God.

Your preferred future will include an upgrade of impact in one or more of those groups. Who is God calling you to influence in this season of life? How might you go about that? These are the simple goals you can set.

When you have prayed this through, go on to fill in the section called "re:FOCUS on People—influencing those around me" within the *Plan to re:FOCUS* section at the back of the book.

PRAY:

Lord, who are you calling me to influence for the kingdom?

Show me how to draw out their destiny through encouragement and blessing.

Amen.

_____

_____

_____

_____

6.6

What have I got?

All that you are, and all you have been given, only reach their potential when they are laid down for God to use.

READ FIRST: EXODUS 3:1–4:4

"So now, go, I am sending you ..." (Exodus 3:10).

That was supposed to be the end of that conversation. At that point Moses was meant to walk off and get to work. But Moses stalled, insisting on arguing about his lack of credentials for the job.

After some dialogue back and forth on the topic, God finally asked Moses, "What is that in your hand?"

You may have already realised by this stage in your walk with God that if He asks a question, it isn't because He doesn't know the answer. In Moses' day, your staff represented your authority and accomplishments, and could also be used as a tool or weapon. Moses' staff represented all Moses brought to the table. And Moses was arguing that it was insufficient for the job.

God wanted Moses to throw it down, to surrender that which was in his hands and give it over to God.

Once surrendered, this same weak rod became the focal point of God's power. It wouldn't have mattered what the rod was made of or represented; all that mattered was that God was going to put His power behind it.

What is in your hand?

Whether it is impressive or seemingly insignificant, when combined with God's empowering grace it becomes enough to change the world. All that matters is that you, like Moses, will cast that which is in your hand before God to use as He sends you.

There are two purpose statements we can use to help you refocus your talents. The first is:

> *I am called to use my talents faithfully—*
> *loving God with all my heart, soul and strength.*

When forming a vision for life that honours this purpose, we are to take into account the various circles of influence we find ourselves in. What do these people need? How can you add kingdom value to their life?

Then we consider the talents and gifts we have, and the core values which drive us to find our sweet-spot of kingdom work.

Our goals change somewhat when we begin with meeting actual needs as our focus, rather than "Where can I use my specific skills and availability?" Our intent becomes finding something fruitful for our hand to do, rather than using the tools we already know we have.

Who knows? God may have other tools for you to learn, and you may have latent capacities that would never see the light of day without you being compelled to try something out of your comfort zone.

What then might your goals be in relation to this purpose statement?

Perhaps you need to focus first on identifying the needs around you? Or, it may be time to allocate specific time to meeting the needs you already see. Perhaps you should invest time in growing your skills more so God can bear more fruit through you.

As is now your habit, pray into this, then fill in the relevant section in the *Plan to re:FOCUS* section at the back of the book.

Our final purpose statement takes the issue of calling beyond the ability for us to give all we have. Our own abilities and strength is limited, God's are not. It is ultimately His power that achieves His ends, and yet His sovereign plan is to work through us to achieve that. Therefore, our final purpose statement is:

> *I am called to work in the power of God—*
> *knowing and using my spiritual gifts.*

The majority of believers are unaware and somewhat non-functional in their God-given spiritual gifts. The ramification of this is that the body of Christ is unable to function in health and power as it should. And whilst it is possible for Christians to work supernaturally outside of their area of gifting, our primary accountability in this regard is to steward well what we have been given.

Any viable vision for a preferred future in this area will entail either discovery, use or growth of your spiritual gifts. There are plentiful, broad-ranging and credible resources available for you to grow in these things. Much can be gained by undertaking these programs as a group or local church.

Since gifts are made to complement each other, at times your own gift profile can be hard to define until you see where those around you are gifted, and where they are in need of what God may have given you.

After you have prayed in to this, fill in the appropriate section of your *Plan to re:FOCUS* at the back of the book.

Pray:

Lord, please reveal to me the talents and gifts you have given me and where they can meet the needs of this world. Like Moses, I willingly lay it all down, so that you may use them through your grace and power.

Amen.

6.6 What have I got?

A FINAL WORD

Your God-given calling is a dynamic and often undefinable journey that is about God-given grace, personal responsibility, interdependent activity and contextual need. The goal of this book was not to define the blueprint for the rest of your life, but to equip you to create a preferred future through any season within it.

I hope you have found it helpful, and just a little challenging.

My prayer for you is that you would grow closer in your union with Christ. And then, within that relationship, find the direction and power you need to fulfil your purpose. I am sure Jesus would say to us, as He did to Peter:

> *"Do you love me? Then feed my sheep".*

Group Session 7

re:FOCUS ON CALLING:

This week of readings (6.1 through 6.6) was all about making a Plan to re:FOCUS.

Q. What was your overall response to the process?

_____

_____

Q. Before looking at the detail of your Plan to re:FOCUS, look again at the purpose statements that were detailed this week:

re:FOCUS on God – knowing Whose I am

- I am called to live as a child of God – abiding closely with Christ, drawing my identity and significance from Him.
- I am called to live as a co-heir with Christ – bearing fruit through the power of His grace working through me.

re:FOCUS on Character – cultivating who I am becoming

- I am called to be Christ-like – the fruit of the Spirit growing tangibly in my life.
- I am called by name – being shaped by God into a unique person who is being not just doing.

re:FOCUS on People – influencing those around me

- I am called to love people – reflecting the heart of God to those around me.
- I am called to lead people – impacting those in my circle of influence.

re:FOCUS on Talent – giving it everything I have got

- I am called to use my talents faithfully – loving God with all my heart, soul and strength.
- I am called to work in the power of God – knowing and using my spiritual gifts.

DISCUSS TOGETHER:

Q. In which two of these aspects of calling have you been strongest historically?

_____

_____

Q. In which two do you struggle most to find focus?

_____

_____

Q. Discuss together your newly developed Plan to re:FOCUS, emphasizing first the plan to address areas where you are not so strong.

_____

_____

_____

CONCLUSION OF THE GROUP MEETING

Discuss together the potential of meeting again regularly to check-up on progress or to revise the participants' Plans.

Pray for each other's journey over the coming weeks and months that they would be able to keep focused on their calling.

Appendix

A Plan to re:FOCUS

Instructions:

For each element of calling, there are two purpose statements (below) to help you re:FOCUS your life. For each, write down a picture of a preferred future (vision) of how that might look in your life for the next foreseeable season. Then, write down some simple goals that will ensure you get there.

re:FOCUS on God: *Knowing Whose I am*

1. I am called to live as a child of God – abiding closely with Christ, drawing my identity and significance from Him.

2. I am called to live as a co-heir with Christ – bearing fruit through the power of His grace working through me.

re:FOCUS on Character: *Cultivating who I am becoming*

3. I am called to be Christ-like – the fruit of the Spirit growing tangibly in my life.

4. I am called by name – being shaped by God into a unique person who is being not just doing.

re:FOCUS on People: *Influencing those around me*

5. I am called to love people – reflecting the heart of God to those around me.

6. I am called to lead people – impacting those in my circle of influence.

re:FOCUS on Talent: *Giving it everything I have got*

7. I am called to use my talents faithfully – loving God with all my heart, soul and strength.

8. I am called to work in the power of God – knowing and using my spiritual gifts.

Download more plans at spiritandtruth.com.au

re:FOCUS on God:
Knowing Whose I am

Purpose #1:

I am called to live as a child of God - abiding closely with Christ, drawing my identity and significance from Him.

Vision:

In my preferred future, this is how I would like my life to look in regard to this purpose:

_____

_____

_____

_____

_____

_____

_____

_____

_____

_____

_____

_____

_____

Goals:

To ensure I realise my vision fully in this area, I will:

Strategy: **Achieved By:**

_____   _____

_____   _____

_____   _____

_____   _____

_____   _____

_____   _____

_____   _____

Purpose #2:

I am called to live as a co-heir with Christ – bearing fruit through the power of His grace working through me.

Vision:

In my preferred future, this is how I would like my life to look in regard to this purpose:

_____

_____

_____

_____

_____

_____

_____

_____

_____

_____

_____

Goals:

To ensure I realise my vision fully in this area, I will:

Strategy: **Achieved By:**

_____   _____

_____   _____

_____   _____

_____   _____

_____   _____

_____   _____

re:FOCUS on Character: *Cultivating who I am becoming*

Purpose #3:

I am called to be Christ-like – the fruit of the Spirit growing tangibly in my life.

Vision:

In my preferred future, this is how I would like my life to look in regard to this purpose:

_____

_____

_____

_____

_____

_____

_____

_____

_____

_____

_____

Goals:

To ensure I realise my vision fully in this area, I will:

Strategy: **Achieved By:**

_____   _____

_____   _____

_____   _____

_____   _____

_____   _____

_____   _____

_____   _____

Purpose #4:

I am called by name – being shaped by God into a unique person who is being not just doing.

Vision:

In my preferred future, this is how I would like my life to look in regard to this purpose:

_____

_____

_____

_____

_____

_____

_____

_____

_____

_____

Goals:

To ensure I realise my vision fully in this area, I will:

Strategy: **Achieved By:**

_____   _____

_____   _____

_____   _____

_____   _____

_____   _____

_____   _____

_____   _____

re:FOCUS on People: *Influencing those around me*

Purpose #5:

I am called to love people – reflecting the heart of God to those around me.

Vision:

In my preferred future, this is how I would like my life to look in regard to this purpose:

_____

_____

_____

_____

_____

Goals:

To ensure I realise my vision fully in this area, I will:

Strategy: **Achieved By:**

Purpose #6:

I am called to lead people – impacting those in my circle of influence.

Vision:

In my preferred future, this is how I would like my life to look in regard to this purpose:

_____

_____

_____

_____

_____

_____

_____

_____

_____

_____

_____

Goals:

To ensure I realise my vision fully in this area, I will:

Strategy: **Achieved By:**

_____   _____

_____   _____

_____   _____

_____   _____

_____   _____

_____   _____

_____   _____

re:FOCUS on Talent: *Giving it everything I have got*

PURPOSE #7:

I am called to use my talents faithfully – loving God with all my heart, soul and strength.

VISION:

In my preferred future, this is how I would like my life to look in regard to this purpose:

_____

_____

_____

_____

_____

_____

_____

_____

_____

_____

_____

_____

Goals:

To ensure I realise my vision fully in this area, I will:

Strategy: **Achieved By:**

_____   _____

_____   _____

_____   _____

_____   _____

_____   _____

_____   _____

_____   _____

Purpose #8:

I am called to work in the power of God –
knowing and using my spiritual gifts

Vision:

In my preferred future, this is how I would like my life to look in regard to this purpose:

Goals:

To ensure I realise my vision fully in this area, I will:

Strategy: **Achieved By:**

_____   _____

_____   _____

_____   _____

_____   _____

_____   _____

_____   _____

_____   _____

Other important areas in which to re:FOCUS

On the pages that follow, list any other areas you feel God would like you to re:FOCUS on.

Area to re:focus:

List any other area you would like to work on:

_____

_____

Vision:

In my preferred future, this is how I would like my life to look in regard to this purpose:

_____

_____

_____

_____

Goals:

To ensure I realise my vision fully in this area, I will:

Strategy **Achieved By:**

_____ _____

_____ _____

_____ _____

Area to re:Focus:

List any other area you would like to work on:

_____

_____

Vision:

In my preferred future, this is how I would like my life to look in regard to this purpose:

_____

_____

_____

_____

Goals:

To ensure I realise my vision fully in this area, I will:

Strategy	**Achieved By:**
_____	_____
_____	_____
_____	_____

Area to re:Focus:

List any other area you would like to work on:

_____

_____

Vision:

In my preferred future, this is how I would like my life to look in regard to this purpose:

_____

_____

_____

_____

Goals:

To ensure I realise my vision fully in this area, I will:

Strategy	**Achieved By:**
_____	_____
_____	_____
_____	_____

Area to re:FOCUS:

List any other area you would like to work on:

_____

_____

Vision:

In my preferred future, this is how I would like my life to look in regard to this purpose:

_____

_____

_____

_____

Goals:

To ensure I realise my vision fully in this area, I will:

Strategy   **Achieved By:**

_____   _____

_____   _____

_____   _____

www.ingramcontent.com/pod-product-compliance
Lightning Source LLC
Chambersburg PA
CBHW071854290426
44110CB00013B/1137